Finding the Fundamentals

*The seven keys that freed me from my prison
and can free you from yours*

By Garry W. Johnson

Covenant Concepts

Covenant Concepts
Post Office Box 12, Eidson, TN 37731
covenantconcepts47@gmail.com
covenantconcepts.org

Finding the Fundamentals
The seven keys that freed me from my prison
and can free you from yours
By Garry W. Johnson

All Covenant Concepts titles, imprints, and distributed lines are
available at special quantity discounts for bulk purchases for sales
promotions, premiums, fundraising, educational, or institutional use.

ISBN: 979-8-9855144-0-7 (paper)
ISBN: 979-8-9855144-1-4 (digital)

Printed in the United States of America

Dedicated to Mr. Joey Robertson

Special thanks to Rachel Ann Blackston and Amberly Walton Groves.

Proceeds from the sale of this book go directly to Covenant Concepts, a 501(c)3 nonprofit organization dedicated to providing prisoners with free educational resources.

Covenant Concepts
P.O. Box 12
Eidson, TN 37731
covenantconcepts.org
covenantconcepts47@gmail.com

Preface

As I sit at my desk thinking about the implications of this book and the 18 long years of my incarceration, I wonder how many people will read the title and become curious enough to order a copy. Since you have, I'll take a few minutes here and tell you a little about myself and why I feel qualified to give you advice.

I started my prison sentence in September of 2000, less than a year after my second marriage began. To say I was the consummate screw-up would be an understatement. My legacy up to that point would include three DUIs, an estranged wife and son, two abandoned businesses, and a trail of broken relationships and burnt bridges. Even before I was incarcerated, I had subjected myself to several forms of prison – some of which I wasn't even aware.

In 2005, after spending four years and seven months in "23-and-1" lockdown, I pled guilty to two counts of Facilitation of First Degree Murder and one count of Aggravated Arson. For my plea, I was awarded a 48-year sentence. But by the time I had my day in court, I had already become familiar with the Fundamentals in this book. As time went on, I learned to more consistently apply these precepts to my everyday life. Through their implementation, I walked out of my physical prison in January of 2018, a very different man.

Today I am an editor at Freebird Publishers, president and founder of the nonprofit that published this book, a freelance writer, a home renovator, and a well-paid consultant at Plastic Innovation in Greeneville, Tennessee. As a result of my first book, I appeared in "Assassin's Flight," the eighth episode of *History's Greatest Escapes with Morgan Freeman* on the History Channel. There I discussed my time at Brushy Mountain and shared my knowledge of James Earl Ray's escape in 1977.

Last year I completed construction on my personal home (a Tiny House … you learn to live in tight places on the inside). I own two trucks, a van, and a Cadillac CTS. I have money in the bank, more work than I can possibly do, and the love and support of my church, family, and friends.

I have the trapping of a full life, just four short years after leaving the penitentiary penniless. And I am debt-free. How? Certainly by no great talent or merit of my own. What success I have achieved in this very short span of time, and the fact that I am free at all, has come directly by implementing these Fundamentals I identified while sitting in the dark hole my previous life had dumped me in to die.

I hope you enjoy the pages ahead as we look at the Seven Fundamentals that produce freedom and true success for everyone who can implement them fully. We will learn what they are, how they affect those who find them, and how you can apply them in whatever situation you find yourself … including your darkest prison.

I pray that you are able to learn them all, apply them fully, and harness the Power they supply. Mastering these Seven Fundamentals will make you *truly successful* and *ultimately free.*

Table of Contents

Fundamental #1

This book contains the fundamentals of success, and success produces freedom. Success in business, finance, family, law – anything that you involve yourself in – all proceed from these Seven Fundamentals. They have produced freedom in my life beyond what I deserve, and they can produce freedom for you.

The fundamentals themselves are fairly obvious, but they are seldom ever directly pursued as a discipline. They are the underlying principles that every successful person has applied. They are universal but often overlooked, and we are going to examine each one, in detail, to learn how you can apply them today and in the future.

So, if these fundamentals are so obvious, if they are so essential, and if every successful person who has achieved success followed them, why do so many people still fail in life? Why are prisons overflowing, death rates soaring, and homelessness an ever-present issue? Why are so many people shoehorned into lives leading nowhere?

Figures on the U.S. prison population are not released consistently, but in 2011, there were 668,800 new admissions into state and federal prisons. Bureau of Justice Statistics figures for 2017 show 1,489,363 prisoners in state and federal prisons in the U.S. When you add territorial prisons, local jails, ICE facilities, military facilities, jails in the Indian Country and juvenile facilities, you get a 2008 figure of 2,418,352 failures to comply with social standards – and that does not count those on probation and parole.

In 2015, it was released that 49 percent of black men in the U.S. have been arrested by age 23; thirty eight percent of white males have been arrested by that same age (*Crime & Delinquency*, as quoted in *Discern*).

Every person who finds himself or herself where I did failed in some way. Some didn't even commit the crime they are incarcerated for (more than you suspect, actually) and many more claim the same. Nonetheless, each prisoner was still in some situation that made it look like they were guilty – and that is still a failure.

Some people can't handle the failure of prison. In my 18 years on the inside, there were numerous suicides and even more "attempts." The year I taught this subject as a course in the penitentiary, I reminded the guys of three men who took their lives on the compound within the previous

> *Some people can't handle the failure of prison.*

12 months. If you have spent any significant time on the inside, you know what I'm talking about. If you ever find yourself on the inside, you'll know soon enough.

And I'm not just talking about in Tennessee. "In California, which has the largest state prison system with about 170,000 inmates, there have been 41 suicides this year, the most in at least six years and a 17 percent increase from 2005 .... In Texas's prison system, which has 169,000 inmates, there have been 24 suicides this year, up from 22 in 2005" ("Inmate suicides linked to solitary," *USA Today*, December 2006). We'll be looking at solitary confinement again shortly and why it is often the end for folks on this dismal road.

Of course, this isn't just a prison issue. The World Health Organization estimates that worldwide, nearly 500,000 people commit suicide each year – almost 1 per minute. Ten times that number engages in non-fatal suicide attempts. This propensity toward ending one's own life reveals a global epidemic of hopelessness and failure innate to the human experience.

But what about those of us living in the most prosperous country the world has ever known? Surely people here are happier than that. Unfortunately, the facts don't bear that out. In the United States suicide is the second most frequent cause of death (after accidents) among 15- to

24-year-olds, which tripled between 1957 and 1992. More suicides (31,000) than homicides (23,000) occur in the United States each year.

Your Future Success

Don't become a statistic. For you and me there is hope. There is another day, another chance to succeed. Even if you are reading this from a prison cell, there are things you can do to make yourself successful. No matter your financial situation, no matter where you find yourself at this moment, today is the day you have been given to make something happen. The wisest ruler of the ancients said:

> *Anyone still alive has something to live for – even a live dog is better than a dead lion.*

I received a letter in the spring of 2014, from Mr. George Kayer, founder of the prisoner resource catalogs *Inmate Shopper* and *The Best 500 Nonprofits*. He later sold these publications to Freebird Publishers, where they are still propagated today. At the time, I was the editor in charge of the prison newsmagazine *Mountain Review*, at Morgan County Correctional Complex, in Wartburg Tennessee (MCCX). We featured his publications in the first quarter 2014 edition of our publication. His letter read, in part:

INMATE SHOPPER
BOX 231
Edna, TX 77957
www.InmateShopper.com
info@InmateShopper.com
A Mountain Review *contributor. A soft-cover book with 200 pages of up-to-date products, services and news. Published three time a year: $17.99.* The Best 500 Non-Profit Organizations for Prisoners: *$14.99. The editor is currently seeking to purchase manuscripts. Send a query letter and outline only. Artists should ask about a free art kit.*

"You ask how do you accomplish what you do from a prison cell? First and foremost know the policies (word-for-word) of your prison. Know what you're allowed to do and what will get you shut down. I work closely with my counselor and the internal security unit. This avoids serious issues before the issue becomes serious.

"Every state has its own policies. In Arizona a prisoner can be published, but he can't be the publisher. We're not allowed to 'run' a business, not allowed direct contact with the public to sell books or ads, but we may have agents handle this. *Inmate Shopper* contracts four separate businesses, five if you include Amazon, to handle the day-to-day business. My focus is writing the next issue, research and responding to an ever-increasing pile of mail" (June 3, 2014).

I was also let in on another prisoner's progress toward reestablishing his place in the business world when he was released. Mr. Tony Lambert put together an extensive business plan for a company he called "ABP Communication, Inc." He used that plan to garner community support for his project.

"I have received an enormous amount of response from the S.B.A. [Small Business Administration], SCORE (Service Core of Retired Executives), and C12 group in regards to my business plan. I have been sending portions of it out as I complete it. Last week the district manager for S.B.A. in Nashville and the Regional Manager for SCORE wrote me and requested the entire packet to present to their members. In addition, the SCORE manager asked if I would be willing to come to Nashville when I get out and make presentations to several organizations there. I, of course, accepted and told him my expected release date" (June 9, 2014).

Both these men set out to pursue a goal while they were yet still incarcerated. Under enormous disadvantage and restriction, they moved forward. How about you? What are you doing right now that is moving you toward your goal? Or do you have a goal? If so, what is it, and is it the *right* goal? How much thought have you given to who you are, where you are, and what you want to be?

The First Fundamental: Set the Right Goal

Where Do You Want to Go?

In order to fix the right goal, you have to be able to define success. You have to know where you want to go in order to get there. Wealthy people all over the world have set their goals on the acquisition of money: but money is not an end in itself.

Legitimately earned, money is a yardstick of services rendered. It is simply a medium of exchange – but it, in itself, is *not* the root of all evil. Money is stored-up effort. You earn money by the services you perform or the products you produce, and then you can exchange that money for someone else's services or products.

> *The use of money is all the advantage there is in having money.*
> *– Benjamin Franklin*

But when we stockpile money, when we save it up and set our desire on it – on having more of it – that's when the problems arise. It is the *love of money*, the desire for riches, the covetousness that can destroy us.

That wise king I quoted earlier also said, "He that loves silver shall not be satisfied with silver; nor he that loves abundance with increase." What he is saying is simply that if money becomes your focus, it will never satisfy – no matter how much of it you have. But he also said in the same book that "money is a defense" (and in some cases, a defense attorney), so it has its use. The problems people have with wealth are due to their attitude – not their money.

And on that note, I want to point out that these Fundamentals are the *key principles* you have to pursue to be successful in life from this point forward. They do not, however, cover every general principle of character, such as honesty, patience, loyalty, courtesy, dependability, punctuality, etc. These are basic qualities of character that you must

5

possess *in addition to* (and eventually, as a result of) the Seven Fundamentals.

Lose the Facade

I have worked on many books written by prisoners and have seen some pretty bad advice in some of them. When I was preparing on the inside to present this information in a class format, I ran across a Prentice Hall book that was just as bad: *Talk Your Way to Success with People*, by J.V. Cerney.

A little research reveals that Cerney was an acupuncturist, who authored a long list of titles dealing with "unorthodox healing methods," as he put it. Among his "medical" books, however, is this one title I had hoped would contain some good advice to offer the men in my class. It is supposed to instruct you on how to become a business success. What it actually contains are directions on becoming a shyster.

In his book, Cerney relates your very personality to the "soft-sell," the idea of selling yourself the way corporations, politicians, and criminals do. His concept is the same as every con man walking the streets today: if you can get people to trust you, you can talk them into anything.

As I read, I could almost envision two criminals dining over plastic food trays discussing what they intended to do the next time they tasted freedom. Of course, Cerney attempts to legitimize his advice by pulling in a specialist. That's what attorneys do when they want a jury to swallow something that just doesn't seem right.

Cerney's "specialist," a public relations man, says you should whitewash (paint over) your true character with the "good guy" image you need people to have of you. You have to appear pleasing to everyone in order to maintain goodwill coming in your direction. You have to phase your marks into sleepwalking, into believing you have their best interest at heart.

His approach is calculated, and he encourages his students to build the necessary "image" they want from pretty pictures and words that have no real meaning. He says you have to build on this fake persona until you perfect the roués. It's all artificial in his program; it's all a put-on for public acceptance. It's just the price of doing business.

Cerney goes into great detail about the "facade," the "snow job" he wants you to "put on" to become a success. He tells his readers that their public relations program has to create an image that shouts:

- I am pure. I am Sir Galahad on a white steed.
- Lean on me. I am thy rod and thy staff. I am clean, and I am good.
- I represent hard work and achievement.
- I move where angels fear to tread. I'm strong.
- I willingly help others in distress.
- My capabilities are at your service.
- I help people to achieve happiness and success.
- I'm honest. I admit when I'm wrong.
- I provide a strong example to follow.
- I am happy and nice to be near.
- I will get along famously with you.
- I understand you and your problems.
- I am respectful and courteous.
- I am socially conscious and broadminded.
- I know my job and am competent.
- I want you to have the best.

In a sense, Cerney is right. You will never be a success if you cannot achieve these very same outward qualities – but you have to do it *legitimately*. It isn't a matter of personality, but of *character*.

He uses the word "facade" in his description of the "snow job" you are advised to pull off. A facade is the false exterior of a building. It is usually the first thing that gives way in an earthquake or an explosion – because it is fake, its purpose is purely aesthetic, it is just for looks. It is "a false, superficial, or artificial appearance or effect" (*Merriam-Webster's 11th Collegiate Dictionary*).

Maximum Exposure

I spent four years and seven months in a 23-and-1, maximum security cell ("max," in prison terminology). In essence, a 6' x 9' solitary cell – just me and the few books they would let me have. I spent my time reading those books, thinking about the life I had led, and studying the psychological attributes of the men who would pass through the unit (many, again and again).

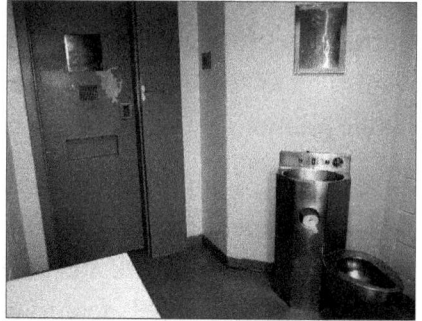

Each cell had a little window in the door and a small opening to insert a food tray. The locks had been disabled on this "pie hole" (also prison slang) and the men could converse and exchange trinkets during their one-hour "out."

The shower was an open box on the bottom floor of the two-tiered security area, and the bottom level had a single phone that placed collect-only calls. The calls were limited to 30 minutes and a prisoner's time out limited to one hour per day.

Under these conditions, you are continuously aware of what each of the other 14 men in your unit are subjected to, because you can see most of it and hear the rest. I observed what the experience did to each of them and contemplated the results.

My conclusions were not typical of the commonly held beliefs. I've heard it said that max brings out the *worst* in people, but it does not. I've also heard it said that tragedies and emergencies bring out the *best* in people, but they don't. Extreme situations reveal what people *already are* – they strip away the facade and reveal what has been underneath all along. And many people cannot handle what they find there. That's why suicide rates are so high in max.

Adversity is like a strong wind. It tears away from us all but the things that cannot be torn, so that we see ourselves as we really are.
– Arthur Golden, American novelist

The lesson to learn here is that no one can hide his or her character forever. It is who you are, and people will always, eventually, reveal to you exactly who they are. Usually all you have to do is listen to them long enough. We can't help it – it always comes out. Out of the abundance of your heart your mouth will eventually speak. … Believe it.

So if anything you read tells you to put on a fake front for any reason, and you follow that advice, your success – if you achieve any at all – will be miserable and short lived. And you'll find yourself one day sitting in a prison cell, or bankruptcy court, or in divorce proceedings, wondering how someone out there saw through your facade.

Becoming Real

After my stint in max and a classification period at Brushy Mountain, my first goal when I arrived at MCCX was to associate with people that demonstrated good character. You see, one of those books I read in max convinced me that if I associated with decent people, it would help me become a decent person.

He that walks with wise men shall be wise:
but a companion of fools shall be destroyed.

Granted, it was a simple goal. But when I first arrived, it was about the only thing I had control over. And it was a start.

My second goal was to try and get back into shape. It was an admirable goal and one we are going to come back to in a later chapter, but it was one I was never able to accomplish on the inside. The First Fundamental did not make me a success in this area, because I did not *continue to apply it.* The Fundamentals are not magic (nothing is), but if you implement them all consistently, you are guaranteed to be a success.

The combination of these first two minor goals had a profound effect on my time at Morgan County. I sought out the only group I was aware of that went to the weight pile *and* the chapel – men who had respectable jobs, who had proven themselves trustworthy to other prisoners and the staff. And that is how I met Roy Ridley.

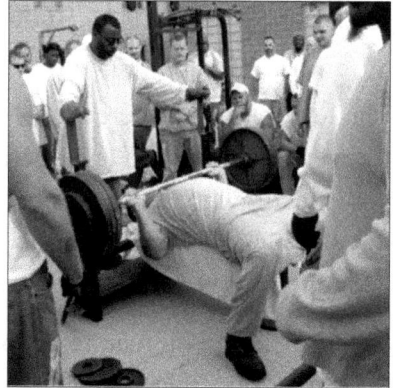

Roy was an editor for the prison newspaper in 2005, and had recently been re-classed to the annex. (Not long after that, a policy change on housing "lifers" brought Roy back to the compound, but at this time he was headed for a new taste of "freedom"). I had been working in my housing unit as a laundry man for almost six months (the minimum time required in Tennessee that new prisoners *must* maintain an "unskilled" position).

Because my first goal was to associate myself with men of high standing, all of my workout partners had good jobs. As they accepted me into their company, they assumed I was capable of working on their level. So when it came time to fill Mr. Ridley's vacant position at the paper, my name was proffered by the group.

With no college training, no literary skills, and a learning disability (I am dyslexic … yeah, a dyslexic writer and editor), I walked directly into one of the most sought-after jobs at the prison – the result of a very simple, very specific, short-term goal and the byproduct of several Fundamentals at play.

So as improbable as it was for me to become a publications writer and editor, you really need to consider the likelihood of achievability before setting goals. Remember, my goal wasn't to become an editor; it was to become a better person. As you implement these Fundamentals in your life, you will often find the result is more than you anticipate. After I became an editor, I had to set new goals to be the best editor I was capable of being. Those new goals paved the way for the book you are reading now.

What Should You Be?

Most people go through life without any goals at all. They never think of having any purpose in life. They are not going anywhere in particular. They are just living day-to-day, waiting to see what happens next.

If you have saved up money for a vacation, you spend a lot of time in planning your trip and anticipating what you'll be doing. You have a definite destination – and all the plans you make are designed to take you to that particular destination – that goal you set out to achieve.

You have to know where you are planning to go, otherwise, how do you ever expect to get there?

But, for some reason, most people have no aim – they are merely the victims of circumstance. They never planned to be in the job or occupation in which they find themselves. They don't live where they do by choice. They don't plan their house or apartment; they just kind of fall into it.

I don't think anyone plans a trip to prison. My excursion (though predictable) was nowhere on my radar. Most people I met in prison didn't even plan the action that

> *Most people I met in prison didn't even plan the action that brought them there.*

11

brought them there. We allowed circumstances to dictate our goals. We drifted right through life, right into jail. We made no effort to master and control our situations.

So how do you assess your situation to fix the right goals? The First Fundamental, I repeat, is to set the *right* goal. There should be an overpowering purpose to your life, but first you have to count the cost and decide if you have what it takes to get you there.

The first step is to make sure your goals are realistic. You have to be brutally honest with yourself about your desire to change and your willingness to do what is necessary. How much will you need to change to achieve the reinvention you desire? Do you have it in you? Consider these crucial questions before you move ahead:

1. *Does your goal match your values?* What exactly is important to you? Is your overall goal truly the most important aspect of your life? If you love the idea of farming but value trips abroad with your family, will you really be able to devote time to husbandry? If your goal doesn't match your values, you'll have less motivation to work toward it, and will feel less fulfilled even if you achieve it.

2. *Does it conflict with other priorities in your life?* If you have decided to become a doctor and you also want a large family, do you have 10 years to spare for medical school, residency, and a fellowship? What about working 12-hour shifts in an emergency room before going home to a new baby? Are you up for that?

3. *Can you gain satisfaction from each step?* Not every aspect of every goal is desirable. Do you want to work in carpentry but don't understand fractions, decimals, and geometry? Is basic math frustrating to you? Think hard before picking up that hammer.

Can you get into a "state of flow" in the area you want to pursue? Athletes refer to it as being "in the zone"; can you achieve focused absorption in the activities surrounding your goal? If so, you'll derive satisfaction from your efforts even if you never fully attain your objective.

4. *Are you sure you want it?* Imagine reaching your goal while considering our tendency to revert to a baseline level of happiness even after success. Will you be happy long-term with the outcome? Ask the people who know you best if they can imagine you in a future where you have obtained your goal.

5. *Is achieving it within your control?* If you are 5' 3" it is not likely you'll end up in the NBA (though point guard Muggsy Bogues did, so nothing is impossible). Will reaching your goal require unlikely conditions, like winning a contest, or overcoming challenges like health or geography? You should be able to plan specific, practical actions to reach your goal.

Now that you have some tips on personal assessment, what methods are necessary to get you where you want to go? You have the desire; you know you can do it – where do you go from here? Are all goals the same, or are there steps to get you where you need to be?

Fundamental #1 is: Set the *right* goal, and all of your goals should be moving you in the *right* direction. Take into consideration these four characteristics that your goals should possess:

1. *Goals must be large.* Shooting for a high mark will create the excitement necessary to accomplish your goals. If your main objective is something in which you have little or no interest, you will likely drift into inaction. The right goal will arouse your ambition. It will be something you desire enough to incite determination; it will push you toward great achievement. The right goal will be so incredible that it will inspire you to new heights and fire you with incentive.

In sports, it is an established fact that athletes perform better against a talented team than they do against a mediocre team. Upsets are forever frustrating bookies, because people can overcome what seem to be insurmountable odds when they want something bad enough. The bigger the goal the more effort it will elicit in you. Niccolò Machiavelli said: *Make no small plans for they have no capacity to stir men's souls.*

2. *Goals must be far-reaching.* Without long-range goals you are likely to be overcome by short-range frustrations. The reason is simple, not everyone is as interested in your success as you are. Occasionally, circumstances or people will get in your way, and that can be frustrating. But long-range goals give you the flexibility to adjust, to overcome setbacks, and to plot an alternate route to your goal. Others can stop you temporarily – only you can stop you permanently.

3. *Goals must be daily.* Sometimes these are referred to as short-range goals. If you don't have daily objectives, you qualify as a dreamer. And dreamers are fine, as long as they are working daily toward realizing their dreams. Charlie Cullen expressed it this way, he said: *The opportunity for greatness does not come cascading down like a torrential Niagara Falls, but rather it comes slowly, one drop at a time.*

   Brian Tracy said: *Every great success is an accumulation of thousands of ordinary efforts no one sees or appreciates.* Daily objectives are the best indicators, and the best builders, of character. This is where dedication, discipline, and determination enter the picture. I eventually learned that I don't have the required determination to exercise for health's sake. When I got out, my goal was to have at least two occupations: One to work my mind, the other my body.

4. *Goals must be unambiguous.* I read an analogy once of trying to start a fire with a magnifying glass – while moving the glass back and forth. It doesn't work. However, if you focus the power of the sun in a single location, you can start a roaring blaze.

   It doesn't matter how smart you are or how much energy you have, if you don't focus it on a specific target and concentrate it there you're never going to accomplish as much as your ability warrants.

And that, my friends, is the key to this Fundamental – your overall focus. For you to be a true success, you must have the right central goal, the right objective, one major aim that is the searing focus of all your other goals … that one big life goal.

The Deeper Question

Few have ever known such a purpose. Down through the centuries, through the millenniums, thinkers and philosophers have pondered and sought in vain to learn whether or not life has a real purpose.

Socrates, Plato, Augustine, and others, have speculated and reasoned, yet the true meaning of life eluded them. This deepest and most important question in life remained to them a mystery – an unsolvable enigma: What is life's goal? What are we doing here?

If one could discover an overall goal – a *definite* purpose for which humans were put on earth – if one could discover a human potential greater than mere temporary existence, then wouldn't *that* purpose be the objective of every soul that draws breath?

But who has ever discovered such an objective as life's true aim? What more is there than to eat, drink, and be merry? Is there nothing greater than to enjoy fleeting status, only to be forgotten by those who come after you?

What is there, after all, to live for? Think on these things as we move forward through the Seven Fundamentals. By the time you have learned and applied them all to your life, you will be fully aware of your life's ultimate goal and how to free yourself from anything that imprisons you.

Begin with the end in mind.
– Stephen Covey

Fundamental #2

I was installing a custom shower in a friend's house in Greeneville, Tennessee. He had been watching me work for quite a while. I had framed in a divider wall, installed sheetrock, reworked the plumbing, and installed a new sink, vanity, and shower pan. I'd been talking to him about the material for the shower walls when he asked, "How did you learn to do all this?"

The question struck me as peculiar, as I had never really thought about it before. I said, "Well, growing up where I did, this is just what we did. We couldn't pay other people to do stuff for us, so we figured out how to do it ourselves." I didn't realize until then how far back my history with the Second Fundamental had gone.

Of course, growing up broke isn't the only reason I do carpentry. Like we discussed in the first chapter, it is one of those activities where I find myself "in the zone." I can lose myself in the work and time can just slip away. Working with my hands and my mind make me happy. Not everyone has that.

Only a third of Americans say they are "very happy," according to a Harris Poll. The US is ranked as the 17th happiest country in the world. *The World Happiness Report* lists another 139 countries that are even *less* happy than we are!

Commissioned by the United Nations, the report ranked the happiest 156 nations based on factors such as life expectancy, perception of corruption, GDP per capita (Gross Domestic Product), personal freedom, social support, and generosity ("Are You Happy?" *Discern*, May/June 2014).

Another survey showed that 33 percent of young Americans between 16 and 25 years of age feel that the future is rather bleak, compared to just 25 percent who feel it's fairly optimistic.

At the time these surveys were conducted, then-president Barack Obama said that it was the best time and place in all of history to be alive. It doesn't seem like his fellow countrymen agreed. With the US deadlocked in a two-party system, half the people in this nation are guaranteed to be miserable about something.

But Barack kind of had a point, though maybe not about the US in particular. For the majority of human history, the average person spent their entire day just trying to figure out how to eat. Now we have the time and money to surf the Internet, get addicted to video games, porn, drugs ... get fat.

How about you? Are you optimistic about the future? If you are not, you should be by the end of this book. By then you'll have the keys to turn your life around, regardless of your current situation. So don't let these statistics and examples I keep bringing up bring you down, because there is a reason for it.

The old adage, "You must learn from the mistakes of others. You can't possibly live long enough to make them all yourself" (credited to Sam Levenson) is great justification for the case-study method.

Following that advice, let's consider the cautionary tale of Jesse Lauriston Livermore, a man who achieved great wealth in his lifetime. A financial trader and investor during the early 20th century, he made most of his money by using a trading technique called "short selling."

Essentially, when a trader expects the market to go down, he can borrow shares and sell them while the price is high. He hopes that by the time he has to return the shares he will be able to purchase them at a lower price so he can make a profit.

During a market panic in 1907, Livermore made about $3 million using this method. He later capitalized on what he learned and amassed an even greater fortune during the great market crash of 1929.

Seeing similarities in conditions to the 1907 run on the market, Livermore began short selling stocks in the months leading up to the crash. He continued to build on those market positions and by the time the October 1929 market crash was complete, Livermore was worth around $100 million.

The strength of the dollar at that time would make his net worth much more than $1 billion, making him one of the 2,755 richest men in the world!

Imagine having a billion dollars. I used to think that if I could just get my hands on some "real money," everything would be great. And I was just thinking $50,000 or $100,000, free and clear. This guy had the equivalent of a *billion* dollars! That's $1,000,000,000.

You know how long it lasted him? Five years.

> *In the blink of an eye, wealth disappears …*
> *it will sprout wings and fly away like an eagle.*

The *Discern* article I got this information from ("Hidden Treasure," March/April 2014) concluded this way: "[B]y 1934, Jesse Livermore was bankrupt. We don't know exactly how his fortune was lost, but we do know he continued to trade the market after 1929, and he suffered the second of two divorces in 1932 (three years after making all that money).

"Livermore slipped into a clinical depression from which he never recovered during the late 1930s. On November 28, 1940, at the age of 63, he committed suicide in a hotel room in New York City" (ibid.).

With a fortune worth a billion dollars, Jesse Livermore couldn't walk away. He had set his goal on the acquisition of money, and money by itself never satisfies, which brings us back to the First Fundamental: Set the Right Goal.

You will learn as you begin to apply the Fundamentals to your personal set of circumstances that they each build one upon another. The information in the first chapter is critical to applying the Second Fundamental.

What Makes You Happy?

We see over and over again that money by itself isn't going to get you there. Nonetheless, whatever you do in life – whatever your goals are – will require you to have an income. Earning an income is going to occupy a large portion of your life, so if you are miserable doing it you are not going to be very happy.

Another article I read included the story of a guy who worked as a software programmer. He was conflicted about the company he worked for because their values didn't line up with his. And he didn't particularly care for office work, being stuck inside day-in and day-out. He was a square peg in a round hole. He wasn't matched well with his career, and he was miserable. He eventually took a pay cut to become a hiking guide.

I knew a lot of guys in prison who worked for Tricor (Tennessee's prison industry program), making better than a hundred to several hundred dollars a month, depending on the industry in their particular prison. Now that doesn't sound like a lot, but when you are housed, fed, and clothed by the state, you can do a lot with $200.

But most of the industry jobs were taxing, either physically or mentally. Then security protocols and the added layer of people to answer to compounded the stress. For many the money wasn't worth it. They traded in the higher pay for state jobs making pennies on the hour, but were far happier people:

> *Do what you love, and you'll never work a day in your life.*
> *– Marc Anthony*

If you find yourself dreading your trip to the office tomorrow, it may be time to reevaluate what you are doing. I took several skills assessments in prison and

> *It may be time to reevaluate what you are doing.*

most matched me well with the things I do today. Recently the system has incorporated the free O-Net Interest Profiler into their programs. Many job-finder websites also link to it, and you can try it out at mynextmove.org/explore/ip.

Interest profilers are useful tools in evaluating yourself, one of the key things you need to be doing as you learn the Fundamentals.

Now let's look at some general guidelines for deciding what type of career you are best suited for and what kind of work will make you the most happy. After all, a job is what you do for a paycheck – a career is what you enjoy doing while getting a paycheck.

Choosing a career that is right for you is no accident. It takes thought, planning, and action! And it is a prerequisite to the Second Fundamental. So, what are your interests?

Your interests are the activities that you enjoy doing for pure fun and pleasure. Your interests may range from participating in physical activities, to creating or communicating. When you work at something you like, it is not like working. Do for pay what you would do for play. Here, in short order, are some other things to consider:

What Are Your Talents? Everyone has talents, but you may not even be aware of what your talents are. A talent is what comes naturally to you without much effort.

What Is Your Personality? This is a key area that is often overlooked when searching for the right career. For example, a person wanted to operate a small restaurant. He had the interest, talent, and prior experience to operate a small restaurant, but he lacked the personality, tact, and temper to work with the public.

If a person would order a hamburger and a glass of water, he would ask the customer, "Are you too cheap to buy a Coke?" Although this person had the interest and the talent, he was simply not suited (personality wise) for this occupation.

About what are you passionate? Passion is the driving force that pulls interests, talents, and personality together. A common characteristic of successful people is that they have a passion for their work. Passion is not a skill or interest, but it is a feeling that comes from the heart! No test or assessment can measure your passion for something.

Some assessments suggest you go through the Yellow Pages from A to Z and make a list of anything in which you are interested. The idea is that you will discover a pattern or spark an area of interest. However, phonebooks are becoming a thing of the past.

The library or a Google search can render several helpful publications you can check out or buy to assess your interests, talents, and personality. These publications, or similar ones, will point you in the right direction: *The Career Assessment Inventory, The General Aptitude Battery Test,* and *The Myers Briggs Personality Indicator.*

Bear in mind that these are only guides, so do not make a career decision based solely on these results. They are only a means to help you gain a better understanding of yourself and provide insight. An effective way to complete your own career assessment is to answer questions such as the following:

- What activities do I do for pure enjoyment?

- What activities cause me to lose track of time?

- What would I do if I had the whole day to myself?

- Do I need close supervision, or can I be self-directed?

- Do I prefer working in a fast-paced environment or working alone?

- What type of books, movies, magazines, or TV shows do I watch or read?

- To what am I naturally drawn?

- If I had the education, training, and qualifications necessary, what profession would I enter?

- If I were financially secure (wealthy) and wanted to work, what type of work would I do?

I had a rare opportunity in prison, being outside of the job market, outside of the daily grind. I had the time to consider what was best for me and what I wanted for the future. I was determined not to just drift back into what I used to know, back into living paycheck to paycheck. I was outside of the "rat race" for a change, and I used that time to make a plan.

Now is *your time* to actually plan for success, this is the time for a change! So you need to decide what is important to you, what you want to do with your life. You need to identify your gifts and your talents, your physical and mental capabilities, and what will make you happy. You need to fix your short-term and long-term goals. And then you need to pursue the Second Fundamental.

The Second Fundamental: Education and Training

What You Must Know to Succeed

Prison can be an extraordinary waste of time and tax dollars for many convicts. Walking into a housing unit, you can find numerous men just sitting around doing nothing … leaning on the ironing board. The regimented routine they are subjected to is embedded with hours of waiting – waiting for chow, yard call, changeover – always waiting for a door to open or a staff member to show up.

Many compound the wasted time with frivolous novels (Westerns, True Crime, Fantasy), card games, "Magic," dominoes. Then there is TV … everyone has a television in their sleeping quarters. When you're locked in with it, you're going to watch it.

And what about you? How much time do you waste on average? According to the A.C. Nielsen Company, the average American watches more than 4 hours of TV each day (or 28 hours/week, or 2 months of nonstop TV-watching per year). In a 65-year life, that person will have spent 9 years glued to the tube. Benjamin Franklin said, "Be always ashamed to catch thyself idle." Are you?

I asked my students, "How much money have you spent this year on commissary, coffee, Christmas packages ... in the last two years, five years, ten years? How many things have you bought that you really didn't need, how many trinkets, how much contraband?"

Think back over the last year. How much money did you spend on things that you really didn't need? How many restaurant visits, when you could have eaten at home; how many new items did you buy that really weren't necessary? How much waste has been in your budget?

> *How much waste has been in your budget?*

Finding the Fundamentals

Now, how much money have you spent on education? What have you done, personally, to advance your skills, your ability to reach your goals? How many books or articles have you read about business, finance, or the field you want to work in? Do you know what field you want to work in?

When was the last time you brushed up on your English skills, or your math? Even basic education is a must for success. If you don't have basic high school skills in every subject, you really need to start there. Could you pass a GED test if you had to take it today? An uneducated person will never master the Fundamentals.

Fortunately, most prisons have a high-school level education program. One of my last jobs on the inside was teaching men the basics to pass the HiSET exam. The U.S. Bureau of Labor Statistics says 40.4 percent of all civilian jobs now require at least a high-school level certification.

Vocational training is the next level of education offered in state and federal facilities, and is a growing area in community colleges. I advised those who took the Fundamentals class not to be afraid to transfer to another facility to pursue classes best suited for the career they wanted. Though 29.7 percent of jobs have no minimum educational requirement, about one-third (33 percent) of the job market now requires pre-employment training (ibid.).

A 2012 report noting the 8,000,000 Baby Boomers turning 65 years of age, said that about 45 percent of the workforce was then planning to retire over the next 5 years. It predicted a tidal wave of retirees and said that existing jobs nationwide shared a huge demand for more education.

Today artificial intelligence, robotics, and other advancements in technology are eating into positions once held by unskilled workers. Complicating matters is the government's push toward socialism, federal unemployment "benefits," and the workforces' unwillingness to work. Ironically, those of us with job skills who are still toeing the line are making more for our abilities because no one else is showing up.

About the time that 2012 report was released, the government started pouring funds into community colleges to up the skilled workforce. Those who took advantage of the training can today write their own check.

College training is the next level of formal education you need to consider. The Bureau reports that 18.5 percent of jobs will require at least a Bachelor's degree, 4.3 percent an Associate's, 2.6 percent a Master's, and 1.4 percent a Professional degree (read "doctor," "lawyer," etc.).

I used to keep a copy of *Preparing for Career Success* in the news office. Typically, prisoners don't have their own office, but the Power of the Fundamentals can do amazing things. My room was located in the back of the prison library, and I maintained books of value for men who were actually seeking to better themselves.

This particular book had an extensive section in it about setting educational goals. Like most prison books, it was outdated but it predicted these to be the largest growth industries requiring a college degree by 2016: 1) Technology 2) Health care and 3) Financial advisers (page 95). Those numbers held true.

Today, according to the search engine Adzuna, the top categories for college grads are 1) Health care and nursing 2) Logistics and warehouse, and 3) Information technology. Since IT is the number one category of new jobs overall (followed by Construction and Drink manufacturing) it's worth taking a look if you are computer-savvy.

Don't be discouraged either about the high cost of post-secondary training. Many are beginning to rebel against the high costs of college tuition, and it may open some doors for those of us who are reluctant to sell a kidney for a college parchment.

Malcolm Gladwell was on 60 Minutes the week I wrote out this curriculum, promoting his new book *David and Goliath*. In it, he advocates for colleges who are less well known but offer comparable educations to Yale and Harvard at much cheaper rates. So when you start looking at programs, don't be discouraged if you cannot afford the fancy-named institutions. It's the accreditation that matters in most fields.

In January of 2016, the year I last offered this program, there were 22 students taking some kind of post-secondary class by correspondence at MCCX, out of 2,000 prisoners! The numbers were low because prisoners don't qualify for student loans, and Pell grants have only recently come back for the incarcerated and under limited conditions.

After saddling my family with over $150,000 in legal bills (the state of Tennessee wanted to execute me at one time), I could not afford college from prison either. Student loans are scaring people out of higher education, and Pell grants won't pay your rent. But if college is a must for the career you want, you need to make it happen. Explore every means at your disposal. There are some creative ways to get around the debt.

Did you know you can take CLEP tests for college credits? The test gauges your knowledge of a subject without requiring that you take a class. All you need is a proctor to administer the test. The Internet is full of ways to learn the material, and major schools like MIT offer open course ware, where entire courses are posted for free. Other programs will give you college credits for work experience.

Whatever you find yourself up against in the battle to educate yourself, *don't give up!* You may be able to secure scholarships, grants, and foundation assistance. Possible sources of educational funding include alumni and other associations, civic and service clubs, church and religious organizations, and private and public foundations. If you don't have the money, look everywhere!

Never Stop Learning

Research the field you are interested in and make sure college is actually a requirement, especially before you go spending large sums of money. A lot of jobs don't require a college education, and even some that do will make an exception for work experience.

I asked a friend who owned a small newspaper how important a journalism degree was when he spoke to applicants. He told me he'd rather hire someone with no degree and work experience (published bylines), than someone coming straight out of school. Having the theories and knowledge is not equivalent to having the experience.

What I'm trying to get across to you is that if you have the drive, you can educate yourself no matter what financial situation you are in, even from a prison cell. I know. I've done it, and you may have to, too.

In prison, you always have access to books. I was surprised at the subjects covered when I checked the library shelves at Morgan County and Northeast Correctional. Most prison libraries are small and stocked with old books, but the range was truly far-reaching. Imagine what your library has. There may be more there than you realize, and it won't cost you a cent.

Next, check into the discount booksellers, like Edward R. Hamilton. Their *Bargain Books* website and catalogs list books on most every subject you can imagine. And they're cheap. If you can't find a book on the specific thing you want to do, look for biographies and autobiographies of people who were successful in the field you want to explore.

If you are incarcerated, there are free book distributors that send used books at no charge to prisoners and other companies that will go on the internet and find you specific titles.

I received a multitude of excellent books for free while I was incarcerated by writing numerous "Books to Prisoners" programs. They send you books by subject matter. In one request, I listed "graphic design" as one of the three subjects and received the book *Designing Multimedia.*

> *I received a multitude of books for free while I was incarcerated.*

It was very outdated when I got it, but it was still in pretty good shape. Now if you know anything about computers, you'll know just how fast information becomes irrelevant. Yet I was still able to learn a great deal from this almost 20-year-old book. Some of that knowledge I still use today in my current job.

Magazines are also a great way to stay current in the field you want to pursue. *Entrepreneur*, *Inc.*, and *Fast Company* are great general business magazines. I paid about $4 or $5 each, for a year subscription, which is less than the cover price for a single issue.

I don't know how they do it, but there are several of these subscription services. Tightwad (P.O. Box 1941, Buford, GA 30515-8941) was the best mail-order subscription seller I found, but there are many more on the Internet.

You can also find specialty magazines in your field of interest at discount prices. I ordered *Print* magazine, which had a publisher's subscription price of $44.96. I purchased the same subscription for $26.

The point is: education is within your reach even if you can't afford college credits or vocational classes. There are still ways to learn, if you will focus your resources in the direction you want to go.

And learning is in itself beneficial. Even with general education, you are literally making yourself smarter, more capable of learning. This will be a necessity in applying the Fundamentals.

Expand Your Mind

Up until the last few years, the scientific community believed that intelligence was a fixed trait – something we're born with, like eye color. It wasn't until recently that we discovered it can be, and is continually, modified over a lifespan. People aren't born stupid; they have to make themselves that way.

Intelligence researcher James Flynn, at the University of Otago in Dunedin, New Zealand, demonstrated that from 1947 to 2002, Americans gained only 4 points on vocabulary and 2 points on math, but a whopping 24 points on testing for similarities. Why? Because we're using our intelligence in different ways. We have altered the balance between the abstract and the concrete through more education and leisure activities.

The discovery of "plasticity" revolutionized brain research by the simple demonstration that: (1) When you exercise your brain, you release natural growth factors and influence neurotransmitters, which enhance your brain's level of performance. (2) The efficiency of cell-to-cell communication via chemical messengers increases. (3) There is a remapping of the functional connections among neurons, as new things are learned new maps are created, or old maps altered. (4) Alternative circuits can be established to compensate for lost or injured areas.

So if you spent your adolescent years killing brain cells like I did, don't fret … you don't need them! Circuits and networks – not the number of nerve cells – are the key to improved function. You have to knit the cells together in new ways by learning more every day. Learning is the means of establishing and maintaining these circuits, like a tree in full bloom gives off branches, twigs, leaves, and blossoms. When you stop learning, it's like winter, and you're only left with the trunk. Be a green tree.

Finding the Fundamentals

By the way, I learned about brain plasticity from a Great Courses class (The Teaching Company) I purchased in prison, while making 50¢ an hour.

At the time, I worked for the system's education department and was starting to realize the effect that learning has on prisoners. Researchers have found that education can improve in-prison behavior and promote reentry success by changing students' thinking patterns and attitudes. Just the act of learning affects the way the brain works and how people interact as a result. I've seen the change.

Studies also indicate that deficits in social cognition (understanding social interactions and the behavior of others), executive cognitive functioning (the ability to plan and implement goal-directed behavior), problem-solving abilities, and self-efficacy are all cognitive issues associated with criminal and antisocial behavior. Learning helps overcome these behaviors, both inside and outside of the system.

By enhancing cognitive abilities and decision making skills, education can help formerly incarcerated people avoid criminal activity and engage in positive behavior. Many scholars believe that education can also increase pro-social attitudes and moral reasoning, improve self-esteem and self-efficacy, and help individuals develop a pro-social identity. This is one of the key understandings on which Covenant Concepts (the publisher of this book) is founded.

These positive developments can serve as a direct counterweight to "prisonization" (what we always referred to as "institutionalization") the process whereby people who are incarcerated become acculturated to the negative values of prison subculture. Some people can't scrub the stink of prison off of them and often find themselves back there as a result.

Goal-driven education therefore is a must, no matter what your current situation is. It is beneficial for you and everyone you come in contact with. It will give you a new perspective and when based on actual truth, you will begin to see the world around you in a much brighter light.

I point that out because learning falsehoods is as dangerous as ignorance. Many of the tragic tales we've studied are based on the lives of highly educated people, but not all education is equal. Learning erroneous precepts won't benefit you any better than setting the wrong goals. You need to be very particular about what you let into your mind. By the time you have mastered these Fundamentals, you will have a gauge for determining everything you really need to know.

Change is the end result of
all true learning.
– Leo Buscaglia

Fundamental #3

I hope by now you have begun to form a plan for applying the first two Fundamentals. If you have, you are on your way to freedom. You have evaluated where you are in life, where you want to go, and mapped out the road you'll need to travel. You've formulated short-term and long-term goals and laid out an education plan that will steadily bringing you closer to your goals.

We have discussed in great detail what we need to consider when setting goals. We have reviewed case studies of people who set the wrong goals, and we have looked at failure rates and the unhappiness that so many have endured by misapplying the first two Fundamentals.

Now we are going to look at another principle that many people refuse to acknowledge. One whose abuse is costing Western society untold billions, and is eating away at this country's solvency. Abuse of this Fundamental is costing individuals their livelihood, their retirement, and frustrating their plans for the future – their plans for success. And it doesn't have to.

Men have been manufacturing remedies for its abuse since the dawn of time. The government has tried to insure it, regulate it, and force you to treat it their way. Entire aisles of bookstores are dedicated to explaining its principles, yet people refuse to heed the advice, and much of the advice isn't worth the paper it's printed on.

Like the first two Fundamentals this one is fairly simple and obvious, but it requires effort to achieve, self-discipline, and determination, and that's why it's so often ignored. The sooner you focus on it, the easier and more likely it will be that you can obtain it, keep it, and benefit from its countless rewards. Mastering the tenets of this Fundamental is a must, if you are to ever be truly free:

The Third Fundamental: Good Health

There are any number of studies you can find that validate the information I'm going to give you here. My first learning in this area came by way of a first-year psychology book one of the Prison Book programs mailed me. One entire chapter was dedicated to stress, coping, and health.

The book cited a 1979 report by the Surgeon General of the United States entitled *Healthy People* (U.S. Public Health Service). The landmark report concluded that improvements in the health of Americans are more likely to result from efforts to prevent disease and promote health than from new drugs and medical technologies. It further cited two additional U.S. government reports, *Healthy People 2010* (2005) and *Health, United States 2004* (2004) as providing strong evidence for that assertion.

Again, none of this is new information. It is simply information that very few people utilize: It's more effective for you to live a healthy lifestyle than it is for a doctor to try to fix you with drugs. If you are on medication, read the "side effects." Often they are worse than the illness you are trying to treat.

Medical advances and sanitary practices have, however, brought under control what used to be major killers. The leading causes of death in the United States and Europe in the early 1900s were influenza, pneumonia, tuberculosis, and gastroenteritis ... one virus, and three infections caused by viruses, bacteria, parasites, or fungi.

Today the main culprits are heart disease and cancer – both fueled by the modern lifestyle. The death rate has almost doubled for heart disease and tripled for cancer since 1900. Even if you believe the conflated numbers of the COVID-19 "pandemic," it still ranked third in 2020 behind cancer and heart disease. Currently we are killing ourselves faster than any virus can hope to.

Heart disease, cancer, and today's other killers (accidents, lower respiratory disease, and stroke) are strongly influenced by *behavioral factors*. Health authorities estimate that half of all cases of early mortality (deaths occurring prior to the life-expectancy age within a culture) from the 10 leading causes of death can be traced to *risky behaviors*. Cigarette smoking, excessive alcohol consumption, insufficient exercise, poor dietary habits, use of illicit drugs, failure to adhere to doctors' instructions, unsafe sex practices, and failure to wear automobile seat belts are the most often cited. Are you participating in any of these risky behaviors?

> *Are you participating in any of these risky behaviors?*

It has gotten so bad that the shrinks even want to intervene. Recognizing the crucial role behavior plays in health maintenance, psychologists have started pouring resources into the field of "health psychology." Having identified many of the psychological and social causes for risky health behaviors, they hope to promote positive changes in such behaviors and initiate "lifestyle interventions."

The belief is that modifying people's health behaviors as a form of illness prevention can reduce medical costs and avert the physical and psychological distress that illness produces. The science beaks it down into two categories – *Health-enhancing behaviors:* healthy dietary habits, safe sexual practices, regular medical checkups, and breast and testicular self-examination; and *Health-impairing behaviors:* tobacco use, fatty diets, a sedentary lifestyle, and unprotected sexual activity.

Psychologists have developed programs that focus on both classes of behavior, but I don't believe you need a psychologist to help you overcome your health issues or even improve your health habits. I do think their observations are something we can benefit from when examining our own willingness – or our unwillingness – to acknowledge problems and follow through on the solutions. But the decision has to be yours (remember that when the fed starts talking about "following the science").

Change does not come easy to people. No one likes to admit they are wrong, and no one likes being told what to do. No one likes changing the diet they've had growing up, the foods they've always loved, the attitudes they've developed about exercise, about sleep – the habits they've indulged for years. And until people are ready to admit that they've been wrong, that there is a problem, there is little chance for growth or change.

Transtheoretical?

How's that for a "five-dollar" word? Don't get too hung up on it, it's just a word psychologists have coined for the processes that underlie behavior change in general, the "six major stages" as they see it. In the 1980s, psychologists James Prochaska and Carlo DiClemente began to study the process that occurs as people modify their thoughts, feelings, and behaviors in positive ways (either on their own or with professional help). Their research resulted in a transtheoretical model:

1) *Precontemplation*: The person does not perceive a health-related problem, denies that it is something that endangers well-being, or feels powerless to change.

Most of us stay at this stage. I have a friend with high cholesterol who "has always eaten like this, but I feel fine."

2) *Contemplation*: The person perceives a problem or the desirability of a behavior change, but has not yet decided to take action.

Thus some smokers are well aware of the health risks of their habit, yet they are not ready to make a decision to quit. Until the perceived benefits of changing outweigh the costs or effort involved, contemplators will not take action.

I've told people the same thing about personal problems they claimed they were incapable of overcoming. Until the guilt and shame of committing a transgression is more powerful than the pleasure the action produces, there is little chance of change.

3) *Preparation*: The person has decided to change the behavior, is making preliminary plans to do so, and may be taking preliminary steps, such as cutting down on the number of cigarettes per day.

I shared with you in chapter one my need to start exercising more. I made an effort over the next few weeks to walk more, but I was only at this preparation stage.

4) *Action*: The person actively begins to engage in behavior change, perhaps stopping smoking altogether. Success at this stage hinges on the behavior-control skills necessary to carry out the plan of action. The action stage requires the greatest commitment of effort and energy.

I finally reached that stage as my back continued to deteriorate in prison. When I taught this as a class, I told those in attendance: "I committed myself to a schedule, to go to the yard and walk every Monday and Friday evening. I set up accountability partners and wrote my intentions down on a calendar. And now you all are involved. If you go to the yard on Monday or Friday night and can't find me, I expect you to ask why." My back did get better.

5) *Maintenance*: The person has been successful in avoiding relapse and has controlled the target behavior for at least 6 months.

This does not mean that the struggle is over. Many people lapse back into their former behavior pattern at various times, but they reinstate their change efforts, as would be expected when one is trying to change deeply ingrained habits. It typically takes smokers three to five cycles through the action stage before they finally beat the habit, and New

Year's resolutions are typically made for 5 or more consecutive years before they are finally carried out successfully (Prochaska et al:, 1994; Schachter, 1982).

6) *Termination*: The change in behavior is so ingrained and under personal control that the original problem behavior will never return.

Now this model does not assume that people go through the stages in a smooth sequence. Longitudinal studies have shown that many people move forward and backward through the stages as they try to change their behavior over time, and many people make repeated efforts to change before they finally succeed.

Phycologists believe that failure at a given stage is likely to occur if the previous stages have not been mastered. So I want you to think about your health situation, or any situation you are facing in life that requires change, and where you may be in this model and what you need to accomplish to move on.

> *Failure at any given stage is likely to occur if the previous stages have not been mastered.*

Next, we're going to look at the three prominent areas of health that we have control over and can change: diet, sleep, and exercise. If you have made it this far in the book, you are probably more intellectually inclined than most and will be able to appreciate how these three prongs of physical health also affect your cognitive abilities. First, we examine what you feed yourself.

Diet

You are what you eat, and you eat what you buy – so stop buying junk! When I walked out of prison, I was physically composed of what I ate and drank while I was on the inside (you don't want to know). Man is physical, part of the physical world, and we convert whatever we eat into energy and living cells. If you want your body to function correctly, to repair itself and perform, you need to put the best fuel into it.

I read a longevity study in National Geographic a few years back, and it compared groups of people in different areas whose members lived the longest. Now the study attributed its findings to several group dynamics, such as community connectivity, environment, and diet. I remember the study so well, because dietary findings have been of great interest to me for several years now.

The group who registered number two on the list, was a close-knit group of Seventh-day Adventists in southern California. For those of you who are unfamiliar with the Adventists, a large majority of them are vegetarians. They believe that God outlined the perfect diet for man in the Garden of Eden when He told Adam:

"See, I have given you every herb that yields seed ... every tree whose fruit yields seed. ... Of every tree of the garden you may freely eat" and later, "thou shalt eat the herb of the field" (Genesis 1:29; 2:16; 3:18). These first three chapters of Genesis reference fruit, grains, nuts, and vegetables as food for mankind.

And the results of this diet speak for themselves. You may not agree with their doctrines, but walking proof for me showed up every Saturday at about 5 o'clock at MCCX: A group of elderly Adventists walked the 700+ yards from the front gate – that's over 2/5 of a mile; almost half a mile – to the chapel for a service, carrying hymnals, instruments, and Bibles. They then walked that distance again, then walked to the annex to conduct another service, before walking back to the parking lot. Their ages ranged from 60s to the late 80s, and there wasn't an overweight person among them.

But as impressive as that is, a vegetarian diet is not what I am advocating here. However, I did advise the prisoners "anytime your chow hall serves fruit or vegetables, you should start by eating all of them you can get and any fruit or vegetable you are offered otherwise – whether you like them or not. ... And stop making wine out of your apples – read this article, then eat them!" Natural foods are hard to come by in the pen.

Fruits and vegetables even make you look better. The chemicals in plant-based foods give your skin a healthier color and many plants provide protein. Unfortunately, plants don't provide enough protein for an ideal diet. That is where meats are essential.

The group who topped the longevity study, was an extended family living on the Japanese island of Okinawa. Their diet was very similar to the popular Mediterranean diet that so many health experts advocate now – high in vegetable content, augmented with plenty of fish, occasional red meat, and limited dairy. This diet will also help you keep the fat off.

Obesity is not only hard on your heart,

Apples Are for Eating! (Not Drinking)

A new study in the *European Journal of Nutrition* suggest that apples, but not apple juice, can help improve your cholesterol profile. After eating about two and a half large apples a day for four weeks, study participants experienced a 7% and 6% dip, respectively, in their LDL (bad) and total cholesterol levels. But when they switched to apple juice (2 cups a day), the same markers increased by 7% and 5%. Processing strips away the apples' fiber, which can bind to the cholesterol and carry it out of your body, according to the study's authors.

Additional studies show apples help fight Alzheimer's, due to a powerful antioxidant, quercetin, that protects brain cells from degenerating in rats and might do the same for humans. You should eat the skin to get the maximum disease-fighting compounds.

A recent Germany study shows that when the natural fiber in apples ferments in the colon (not in a bag under your bunk), it produces chemicals that help fight the formation of cancer cells.

– with reporting by Reader's Digest *and* Men's Health

it is hard on your brain as well. Controlling your weight is a way of improving your cognitive function, which is essential to fully implementing the Fundamentals.

How much caloric restriction is necessary? The class of foods chosen is less important than the number of calories eaten. Animal research over the past 65 years has shown that the rate of degenerative disease is slowed by caloric restriction, which means a balanced reduction of protein, fat, and carbs without reduction of nutrient content.

Now this may be hard to pull off, but you know what junk you are buying. I remember the "reward" deals the administration at Northeast Correctional (NECX) used to give, "allowing" us to buy doughnuts after passing an inspection. I told the guys not to fall for it ... it's all just empty calories. It's been proven that animals that eat 35 percent fewer calories live 35 percent longer. They are also healthier and have enhanced cognitive performance.

The National Institute of Aging has published a study showing that a 25 percent caloric restriction resulted in a lowering of body temperature and insulin levels, which suggest that such a diet works for the human animal as well. But a key issue here is that few people would be willing to conform to such a diet. Fortunately, keeping calories low enough to prevent obesity may be enough.

Diets high in saturated fats lead to animals' underperformance on tests of memory and tests of reinforcing rewards (e.g., pressing a button to get food). Likewise, reduction in fats and "empty calories" will improve your memory and brain function.

State and Federal prisons have numerous programs on addiction, but did you know that addiction and obesity are linked together? High-fat, high-calorie diets decrease the responsiveness of the brain's pleasure centers. Changes in brain chemistry involving dopamine and opioids lead to compulsive eating patterns. Obesity and addiction may result from similar maladaptations in the brain's reward systems.

Losing weight is never easy, but if your BMI (body mass index) is topped out, you need to put forth the effort to get it down. It won't be easy, but it is worth the effort due to the effects on the brain and the heart. Start by eliminating from your diet those foods that can be proven to cause harm:

Trans fats: They are fats that are formed when liquid oils are transformed into solid fats by adding hydrogen to vegetable oil. Avoid hydrogenated and partially hydrogenated foods. Fast foods (also a favorite "reward" in prison) are the worst: fried chicken, fried fish, biscuits, French fries, potato chips, doughnuts, and muffins.

Smoked and cured meats: From bacon to summer sausage (or that chow hall sausage "patty"), you need to pass on cured meats in any form – they've been linked to cancer, cardiovascular disease, high blood pressure, and migraines. Plus, they're packed with artery-clogging greases: Regulations allow up to 50 percent (by weight) of fresh pork sausage to be fat!

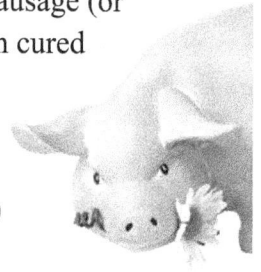

Soft drinks: Stick to a cup of coffee for your afternoon boost. Seemingly harmless caffeinated beverages are often loaded with sugar, and sugar causes a host of health problems. A 20-ounce Coca-Cola contains 600 ml of sugar … that's 15 teaspoons!

White rice: Skip refined grains altogether. A 17 percent higher risk of diabetes is associated with eating five or more servings of white rice per week, compared with eating white rice less than once a month. In fact, all refined foods should be listed here, like white sugar, white pasta, and white bread. Each has been stripped of its original nutrient content and fiber – none of them are good for you.

Fake butter: Whether spread on bread or nuked in microwave popcorn, many butter substitutes and flavorings contain diacetyl-based chemicals, which may harm brain cells. Diacetyl promotes the protein clumps in the brain that mark Alzheimer's disease, according to scientists at the

University of Minnesota. Researcher Ashhish Vartak, PhD, says that the study is preliminary, but he and his colleagues have started avoiding diacetyl by snacking on unflavored popcorn (they add salt or herbs).

Substitute these items in your diet with fruits, vegetables, chicken, fish, whole-grain breads, and green leafy vegetables. Try finding and eating more of these:

Sweet Potatoes: A nutritional superstar, they are loaded with carotenoids, and are a good source of potassium and fiber. For an added treat, toss a few sweet potato wedges in a frying pan with a bit of olive oil and roast until tender and lightly browned. Spice with chili pepper, cilantro, cinnamon, or coconut to add a touch of flavor.

Frozen broccoli: Surprise! Frozen varieties may contain 35 percent more beta-carotene by weight than fresh broccoli that's shipped across the country. Plus, the sulforaphane in broccoli may help your body fight off infections that inflame the lungs and arteries. Finally, broccoli's high level of vitamin C helps create collagen, which keeps skin healthy, firm, and glowing.

Hot peppers: The heat source in these fiery bites, capsaicin, may help prevent the blood clots that lead to a heart attack and stroke. Plus, eating hot peppers can provide temporary relief from nasal and sinus congestion – and even provide a quick lift to your metabolism.

Peanuts: They are as popular as they are healthy. An excellent plant-based source of protein and high in various vitamins, minerals, and plant compounds, peanuts have been available in every correctional facility I've been housed. They can be useful as a part of a weight loss diet and may reduce your risk of both heart disease and gallstones.

Spinach: More popular these days in the average American diet than it was 40 years ago when Popeye was singing its praises! It is one of the

healthiest foods you can eat, and its low in fat and
cholesterol. It is also high in protein and fiber, zinc
and iron, niacin, calcium, iron, magnesium, copper,
potassium, manganese, and loaded with vitamins.
Plus, hello flavonoids! This leafy green is packed
with good stuff for the gut, brain, cardiovascular
system, and blood pressure. Plus, it is versatile!
Do a little research, and you'll discover that
spinach works in a variety of hot and cold dishes. It
will, in fact, help you to get big and strong.

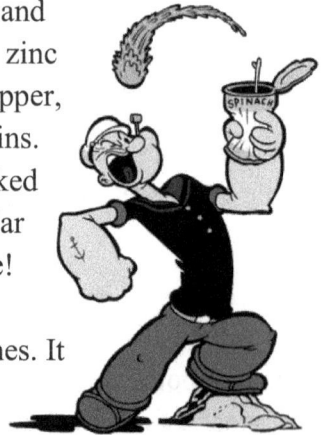

Orange pith: You already know that oranges
are a great source of vitamin C, but eat as much as you can of the pith –
the spongy white layer between the zest and the pulp that clings to a
peeled orange – too. Although bitter, the pith stores a good amount of the
fruit's fiber and antioxidants. (Also be sure to brush your teeth *before*
you have that breakfast orange. Brushing after consuming acidic foods
can cause tooth erosion.)

Beets: I didn't see these often on the inside, but during certain seasons
they were plentiful. Nutrient-packed beets can sharpen your mind. They
produce nitric acid, which helps increase blood flow throughout your
body – including the areas of the brain that are associated with
degeneration and dementia. They are most effective when eaten raw,
grated in a salad.

Fish: These provide an important food source of omega-3 unsaturated
fatty acids. Omega-3s are found in oily fish like mackerel, salmon, trout,
herring, and sardines. They improve mental clarity and may decrease the
likelihood of depression. Two servings a week is probably sufficient, but
not all fish is the same. The debate today is over which has a better
nutritional value: wild fish or farmed fish (chiefly salmon). The
argument seems obscured by environmentalists who prefer you eat from
the company-stocked pool. I don't want to get too deep in the weeds

here, but remember that wild salmon eat what is in their natural environment, while farmed salmon are given a processed, high fat, high protein diet to make them larger for the market. Which do you think would be healthier?

Taming That Funky Fish

The benefits of eating fish, at least the fish we can purchase (salmon, tuna, sardines and, from that recently-contracted "Christmas" package, mackerel) outweighs any risks from potentially high levels of mercury and other contaminants found in some species (avoid shark, swordfish, *king* mackerel and tilefish, especially). Researchers found that just 3 ounces of farmed salmon or 6 ounces of mackerel a week reduces the risk of death from heart disease by 36% (*Journal of the American Medical Association)*.

The Institute of Medicine, which advises Congress on matters of health and science, says fish additionally helps develop the brains and eyes of children and recommends two 3-ounce servings of clean fish a week for everyone. These fish are an important source of unsaturated fatty acids and omega3s, which improve mental clarity and may decrease the likelihood of depression (*Optimizing Brain Fitness,* The Great Courses).

Despite the benefits of fish, many prisoners cannot stand the taste, especially of sardines (although they rank very high in nutrition). Here is a recipe I've found that works great for sardines, tuna and mackerel (I'll share my "salmon stew" in an upcoming issue).

Ingredients:

1 Ramen noodle soup (chicken flavor)
1 3-5 ounce pack of fish (not salmon)
1 kosher dill pickle
3 packs of Jalapeño peppers slices
1 large dollop of mayonnaise

Soak the noodles in a full bowl of boiling water. Set aside. Finely dice the pickle and peppers, put in a tumbler with the pickle juice and mix. Drain water from the noodles (they don't have to be hot), mix in the seasoning pack, the fish, the mayonnaise and three to five heaping spoons of the diced pickle and peppers. If you're using sardines, chop them up with a fork or spoon. Makes one full bowl, with enough pickle and peppers left over for at least two more meals. *MR*

I read a book several years back called *The Maker's Diet* written by a guy who had advanced Crohn's disease. Crohn's is characterized by chronic inflammation of the digestive tract, and in his case it was killing him. The photos of this teenager in the opening chapters of the book looked like someone straight out of a World War II concentration camp.

Fortunately for him, his father was relentless in trying to find his son some relief. After trying literally hundreds of different dietary plans, they came across a guy advocating the Mediterranean diet before it became such a big deal. That was the only diet that started to reverse the kid's symptoms.

But it wasn't until they imposed the guidelines found in Leviticus 11 and Deuteronomy 14 in the Christian Bible, on top of the Mediterranean plan, that the patient began to get stronger and started to recover from his illness.

In essence, *The Maker's Diet* advocated the same Biblical guidelines that Jesus, as a first-century Jew, would have followed, along with the wholefoods approach people enjoyed before we started processing most everything we eat (white flour, white rice, refined sugar). The guy's Crohn's was in full remission by the end of the book. In the after photos, he looked like a different person: healthy skin, muscle tone, tan – the before and after pictures were astounding.

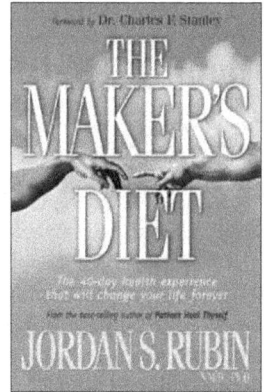

Now you're not going to get whole-grain bread in prison like the Bible mentions, or long-grain rice … and dates and wine were definitely out of the question. But I was able to avoid what the Bible classifies as "unclean foods" and the processed junk sold by the commissary vendor.

I know people get weird when you mention religious doctrines concerning what they eat, but prison policies helped me implement a lot of this. At the very least, research how the medical evidence lines up with what the Bible says, and adjust what is under your control accordingly. I'll include information at the end of the book for a booklet that goes deeper into the medical research concerning these foods, as well as the Biblical guidelines.

"Eat that which is good ..." Isaiah 55:2

As for my commissary, in Tennessee you could buy refried beans and peanuts, which are loaded with good plant protein. One bag of peanuts has 25 percent of all the protein you need for a whole day. Add a meal with two Folgers jar lids of refried beans (the closest thing I had to a "cup"), and you are well over 50 percent of what you need for a 2,000 calorie diet.

Chicken, salmon, tuna, and sardines are just about the best meat products on the market, as far as your health is concerned. The three fish products on my commissary were listed among the five best natural sources of omega-3 unsaturated fatty acids. And, not coincidentally, all the fish listed in that research – as well as chicken – are classified as "clean" meats in the Biblical text.

All the fish listed in that research are classified as "clean" in the Biblical text.

Short of mustard and trail mix, there's wasn't much else Tennessee sold to their captives that had any redeeming value. Even the breakfast drinks and granola bars were loaded with so much sugar, they offer little benefit. But once a year, through the "Package Program" (at Christmas) I had the opportunity to load up on nutritious foods. I spent whatever I could each year on clean fish, olives, and tree nuts – all of which are very good for you.

So once you have cleaned up your diet, started losing excess weight, and restricted your caloric intake, what else does the body need to function correctly? What else should you do to make sure health issues don't limit your freedom?

Sleep

A lot of people view sleep as pointless downtime, especially in this day and age. People who are driven to succeed tend to hate downtime and disapprove of sleep and naps. As a result, folks in the rat-race are sleeping 45 minutes less per day than a generation ago (and no one is waking them up for "count"). But sufficient sleep (including naps) is actually not a waste of time. Sleep is essential to good physical and mental health. It's also essential to good productivity.

Sleep-impaired judgment and performance are as disabling as alcohol intoxication. The more people sleep, the better they perform. The top students at any school sleep more than their compatriots (and you are in school now).

"In vain do you rise up early, and stay up late"

In 2008, the National Sleep Foundation found that U.S. workers are suffering from a dramatic lack of sleep, costing companies billions of dollars in lost productivity. Nearly three in ten workers became very sleepy or fell asleep at work during the month of the study (*USA Today*, March 2003).

Study Says the Morning Sun Helps You Lose the Buns

To maximize your chances of fighting flab, new research offers some simple advice: Wake up early and go outside.

People who loaded up on light exposure at the beginning of the day were most likely to have a lower body mass index, according to a study published in April in the journal *PLOS ONE*. That relationship between morning light and BMI was independent of how many calories the study participants consumed.

It may sound crazy, but there is sound scientific evidence to back up the link. Circadian rhythm plays an important role in regulating metabolism, and studies have shown exposure to light can influence body fat and the hormones that regulate appetite.

In one study, for instance, sleep-deprived subjects whose levels of the hormone leptin and ghrelin were out of whack saw those levels improve after being exposed to light for two hours after waking up. In another study, obese women who were exposed to bright light for at least 45 minutes between 6 and 9 a.m. dropped some of their body fat after three weeks.

– Los Angeles Times

Chronic sleep loss also reduces the body's resistance to infection. Studies have shown that, in general, when healthy people miss sleep, their bodies produce fewer cells to fight off infection. Experiments on volunteers subjected them to two or three days of sleep deprivation. Afterwards, there was a significant reduction in various aspects of their overall immune function.

Metabolism also slows down as a result of not getting enough sleep, causing weight gain and a risk of type 2 diabetes. When the body is tired, it reduces your fat cells' ability to respond properly to the hormone insulin, which is critical for regulating energy storage and use (*Annals of Internal Medicine*).

Missing sleep also messes with your mind. We consolidate memories, fixing them in our minds both when we are awake

> *Missing sleep messes with your mind.*

and asleep. But enhancement, which is improving upon what you have learned, occurs during sleep; it's what's called an "off-line effect."

This all has practical implications: You can improve your learning by scheduling sleep. The initial consolidation of something new takes about 6 hours, so don't take up a new activity within that same framework. Sleep on what you've learned; your brain circuits will be refreshed.

Consequently, a power nap is nearly as powerful a skill memory enhancer as a night's sleep. For instance, finger dexterity increases 16 percent after a nap. Learning facts, words, concepts, and creativity are also improved. But there's a paradox involved in establishing the nap habit: You can't force it. The more you try to force yourself to sleep, the more awake you will be.

And naps must be short so as not to interfere with nighttime sleeping. Sleep for no longer than 30 minutes: The ideal nap duration is around 20 minutes. This helps prevent the body from reaching the deeper stages of sleep, and it keeps a person from waking up feeling groggy. Think of naps as an opportunity for memory consolidation and enhancement, refreshing the brain circuits involved in learning and memory, and an easy way to power down and increase your creative powers.

That being said, don't overdo it. Getting too much sleep may be just as toxic to health as sleeping too little. Slothfulness is a killer, too.

Researchers at Brigham and Women's Hospital in Boston examined more than 20 years of data from over 15,000 participants in the Nurse's Health Study and found that regularly sleeping two hours more or less than seven hours a night was equivalent to two years of brain aging (as measured on standard memory tests). The cognitive effects were also present when sleep habits changed by two hours a night or more as participants got older.

Of course, the *quality* of your sleep might not be great either – mine certainly wasn't in the pen. One of the worst parts of prison for me was my mat. Fatigue is rampant among prisoners, and the causes are not always apparent. If you're getting enough sleep and still feel exhausted all the time, the quality of your sleep may be the problem.

Sleep apnea, restless-leg syndrome, and noisy neighbors are all problems you may have to deal with. Low testosterone levels can cause this too. Many prisoners have thinning or no hair. Stress causes testosterone levels to drop and low testosterone causes your hair to fall out and fatigue. These are all things you need to consider if you are feeling sluggish on a regular basis.

So here is the take-away: For optimal mental and physical health, get seven hours of quality sleep each night (however long that takes) and one 20-minute nap each day after scheduled learning. This may be difficult, depending on how your day is structured, but the benefits are worth the effort in scheduling.

"The sleep of a laboring man is sweet"

Exercise

A sedentary lifestyle is a significant risk factor for health problems, including coronary heart disease and obesity. Despite this widely publicized fact, about 70 percent of Americans are inactive (Baum et al., 1997; Ehrman, 2003). As fewer people now engage in

Americans <u>not</u> involved in active sports, by age:

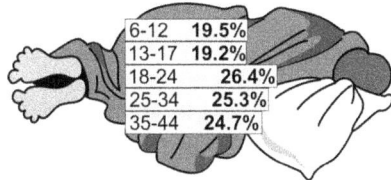

6-12	19.5%
13-17	19.2%
18-24	26.4%
25-34	25.3%
35-44	24.7%

Source: PHIT America, based on a 2012 survey of 41,000 Americans asked about 104 sports or physical activities.

vigorous manual labor, inactivity has helped double the rate of obesity since 1900, despite a 10 percent decrease in daily caloric intake over the same period (Friedman & DiMatteo, 1989).

In fact, "exercise" for its own sake is really a fairly new concept. Up until the 1900s most people walked everywhere they went and worked hard every day just to eat. Additional exercise wasn't something people needed before we became a consumer society.

"In the sweat of your face you shall eat bread"

It may also explain why the ancients were so much smarter than we are. Older adults with a history of exercise have better-preserved brains than those who have not exercised.

The benefits include increased blood flow and new capillaries around neurons, increased production of new neurons and more interconnections between neurons, and the protection of dopamine neurons from neurotoxins.

Exercise also leads to elevations in nerve growth factor and preferentially enhances prefrontal executive processes. The positive balance in neurotransmitters brought about by exercise can even function just like an antidepressant. A daily 1-mile walk reduces dementia risk by 50 percent.

To go a step further, try aerobic exercise. This is sustained activity, such as jogging and jumping jacks, which elevates the heart rate and increases the body's need for oxygen. This kind of exercise has many physical benefits.

In a body that is well conditioned by regular aerobic exercise, the heart beats more slowly and efficiently, oxygen is better utilized, slow-wave sleep increases, cholesterol levels may be reduced, faster physiological adaptation to stressors occurs, and more calories are burned (Baum & Posluszny, 1999; deGeus, 2000).

A study that followed 17,000 Harvard undergraduates into middle age revealed that death rates were one quarter to one third lower among moderate exercisers than among those in a less active group of the same age.

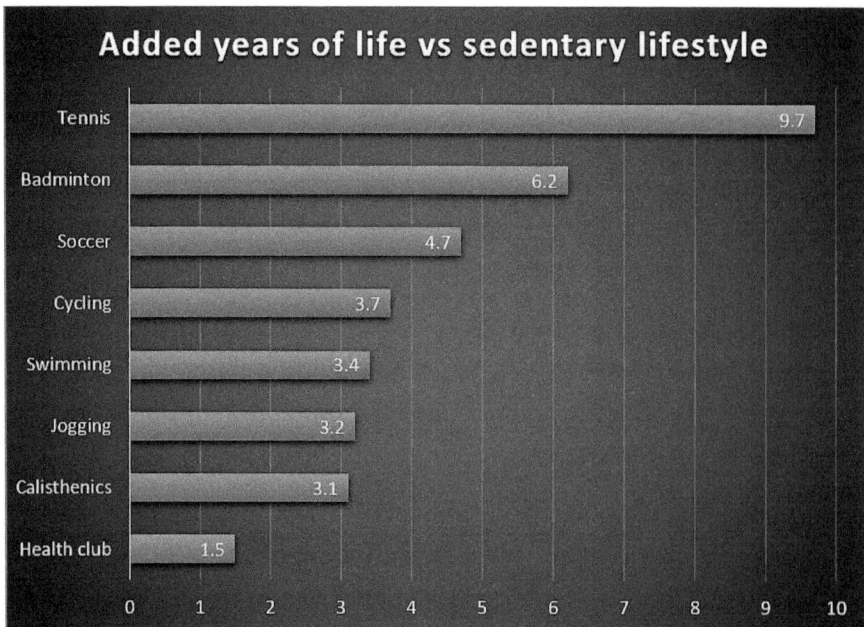

Added years of life vs sedentary lifestyle

Activity	Added years
Tennis	9.7
Badminton	6.2
Soccer	4.7
Cycling	3.7
Swimming	3.4
Jogging	3.2
Calisthenics	3.1
Health club	1.5

Surprisingly, perhaps, extremely high levels of exercise were not associated with enhanced health. Instead, moderate exercise (burning 2,000 to 3,500 calories per week) on a regular basis produced the best health benefits (Paffenbarger et al., 1986). Performing at 70 to 85 percent of maximal heart rate nonstop for 15 minutes three times a week significantly reduces risk for coronary heart disease (Dishman, 1982). Such exercise also has positive psychological effects, reducing depression and anxiety (Morgan, 1997).

Findings such as these have inspired behavioral interventions designed to promote regular exercise. Typically, these programs have an educational component that addresses the benefits of regular exercise and the best ways to exercise.

Yet despite the demonstrated benefits of regular exercise and the educational programs, people in developed countries have a strong tendency either to avoid or discontinue it after a short period. In the United States, for example, only one fourth of the adult population exercises at levels high enough to maintain cardiorespiratory fitness and reduce the risk of premature death (Ehrman, 2003).

When employers offer exercise programs to their employees, it is uncommon for more than 30 percent to participate, and dropout rates of 50 percent within 6 months are found in virtually all exercise programs that have been studied (Chenoweth, 2002; Dishman, 1994).

So you need to focus on the components of behavior change which are necessary to follow through, such as setting goals, writing explicit contracts that specify an exercise regimen, monitoring your exercise behavior on a daily basis, and increasing social support by choosing an exercise partner or group. People who are able to persist for three to six months are likely to continue and develop exercise as a healthy habit (McAuley, 1992). How about you?

No Time Like the Present

As with all the Fundamentals, you have to start toward your fitness goals by believing that you can accomplish what you are setting out to do. No matter how long the odds, you must remember that people just like you have made incredible transformations, so there is no reason you can't, too. Here are three steps you can take to help you believe in your potential and then live up to it:

Announce it: When you make a commitment to improve your fitness, get it out there! Tell your friends, family, and coworkers, put it on your wall (not during inspections). Rally your support system, and let them know you're making the journey. Remember me telling my class and asking them to check up on me?

Prepare: Do your best to surround yourself with things you need to be successful, and eliminate anything that could threaten your success. For example, clean out your pantry or commissary sack and restock it with healthy snacks. Don't buy any more junk, and research food and activities that will improve any medical issues you may be facing.

Follow the "SMART" acronym: "S" stands for specific – know exactly what it is you want to achieve. "M" is measurable – make sure your goal is quantifiable. You must be able to keep track of pounds, inches, blood pressure, or anything else that allows you to see progress. "A" means attainable – your goal must be realistic. "R" is relevant – your goal must be a priority and have significant meaning to you. "T" stands for time sensitive – your goal should have a firm timeline attached to it.

The pursuit of this Fundamental is life long and will change as your body ages. It requires research, effort, and a long-range commitment to taking the best care you can of what you have to work with. It's a moving target, but the more you know, the better chance you have at staying on top of it. If your body fails, your pursuit of freedom is over.

Are you ready? Is your freedom and future success important enough to you to pursue this Fundamental as if your life depended on it? Will you work to maximize your diet, regulate your exercise, and develop the best of sleep habits? Are your goals high enough? Is your will strong enough to follow through? Do you have what it takes to master the Third Fundamental?

> *The doctor of the future will give no medicine, but will involve the patient in the proper use of food, fresh air, and exercise."*
> *– Thomas A. Edison*

Covenant Concepts

Fundamental #4

So let's say you had developed yourself a goal. Let's say, hypothetically, that you possess the motivation to achieve your goal, and with your goal in mind you educated yourself to reach said goal. You gain the experience necessary, and you kept yourself in excellent health. Now you're ready to get started toward achieving your goal.

Sounds like you've about got it licked, right? Sorry – no.

As important as these first three Fundamentals are, life always has surprises in store. I had all this licked back in my 30's, then *BANG!* There I was, in jail … a much unexpected complication. You might be mired in something like that too. But I did have something in my favor; I already had a little experience with the Fourth Fundamental.

In August of 2000, I was on the verge of opening my first legitimate sign company. I had set a goal to go into business for myself. Over the course of my life I had obtained an education in sign manufacturing, screen printing, and computer graphics.

I worked for my dad for seven years doing industrial screen printing. I would set up the machines, shoot the screens, oversee the runs, mix the inks, rack, stack, and box the product.

I've printed poster runs up in the tens of thousands for department and grocery stores; bumper stickers for more causes than I can name; door signs for motel rooms, colleges, office buildings; real estate signs; political campaigns; T-shirts; hats; cups; I have even screen printed directly on the side of vehicles and in the center of dinner plates.

After my dad retired and moved to Tennessee, I worked for my uncle for about a year before going into home and commercial renovations – contract remodeling. My uncle was an alcoholic and eventually destroyed the business. But I didn't want to work against the family company, and found remodeling work an easy shell for hiding drug money. Of course, I quit paying taxes around the following year, so I don't guess that really mattered either.

A couple of years later, I moved to Tennessee myself. I was on the brink of getting busted in Georgia; and even in my deplorable condition, I could see the walls closing in. So I finally gave up drug dealing, changed states, and began contracting work out from local sign companies. Having done installation work as a kid and working with the designers, sign painters, and computer graphic guys that worked for my dad, it wasn't hard to expand into those areas.

I managed to talk my way into a couple of jobs and picked up some new experience. I learned how to construct electrical signs, channel letters; run the graphics programs and vinyl plotter while doing this contract work in Sevierville and Knoxville, Tennessee. I honed my skills while working for these other businesses.

So in 1999, I found myself with all the skills, all the education in my chosen field of work. I had finally set a goal – to open a legitimate, licensed, tax-paying sign business. I was in good health, having done construction and installation work for the past several years. But with all this in line, with these three major Fundamentals firmly in my grasp, I still had an obstacle to overcome: I didn't have any money.

That was my Achilles heel: no real money, no credit, and no track record of business success. Now I had to begin my development of the Fourth Fundamental.

The Forth Fundamental: Resourcefulness

Resourceful is an adjective, it is a word that modifies a noun. If you are resourceful, you are, "full of resource; able to deal promptly and effectively with problems, difficulties, etc; able to meet situations:

capable of devising ways and means; able to use the means at one's disposal to meet situations effectively."

The noun, resourcefulness, is "The ability and the means to meet situations effectively."

So how do you acquire the means? One way to acquire resources is through networking. In the next chapter, we'll discuss how everyone in prison is interconnected, but for now you need to realize that people can be your most valuable resource or another big obstacle – the choice is yours.

No Man is an Island

If you choose to surround yourself with quality people, you'll soon find that your ability to function has greatly improved. But they can't be mined like minerals: you have to be able to make sincere and legitimate connections.

Through my contracting work in Tennessee, I was able to network with several successful business people. They got to know me through my work, the product of my years in the sign and construction business (education, preparation), my ability to climb the scaffoldings and persevere in the sun (good health), and my knack for doing things on time, reaching my short-term goals.

A good name is rather to be chosen than great riches,
and loving favor rather than silver and gold.

One of the guys I worked for owned several gift shops, one in Pigeon Forge, one in Gatlinburg, and several more in Cherokee, North Carolina. Through his experience working with me, he knew that I would follow through with what I said.

After completing a large electrical sign for his Gatlinburg store, he agreed to help me finance the equipment to open my own business. We worked out a deal on producing banners for his stores, and he fronted (loaned) me the funds to purchase the computer, plotter, equipment, and materials. That's how my second business, Grafixx Signs, came into existence.

Steve Lewis (a prisoner) let me borrow this list of rules his dad sent him from Dale Carnegie's classic book, *How to Win Friends and Influence People*. This is Carnegie's summary of "Six Ways to Make People Like You."

Rule 1: Become genuinely interested in other people.

Rule 2: Smile.

Rule 3: Remember that a man's name is to him the sweetest and most important sound in any language.

This has always been a problem for me. I am not good with names. So I picked up a trick from my dad. He would always keep a pad of paper on his desk by the phone, and as soon as the customer said who he was, my dad would write his name down. Then he would use it repeatedly in the conversation.

Rule 4: Be a good listener. Encourage others to talk about themselves.

This has a two-fold benefit. People love to talk about themselves, and that will make them like you. But you'll also learn more by listening than talking. I have said this

If you listen to people long enough, they will tell you exactly who they are.

repeatedly, I may have even said it in this book already: "If you listen to people long enough, they will tell you exactly who they are." You cannot hide your character from someone who is willing to listen to you. Out of the abundance of your heart your mouth will speak.

Rule 5: Talk in terms of the other man's interests.
Rule 6: Make the other person feel important – and do it sincerely."

Genuineness and sincerity is the difference between what Dale Carnegie taught and the book we reviewed in Chapter 1, by J.V. Cerney. It's the difference between a shyster and a success.

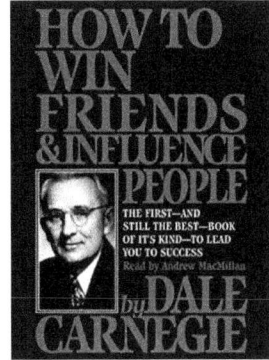

Order yourself a copy of *How To Win Friends and Influence People*; it is well worth your time and money. It is a classic in the field of self-help, and Carnegie presents legitimate strategies for building personal and business relationships. We will extract more from his book as we go on.

*Friends are those rare people who ask how we are
and then wait to hear the answer. – Ed Cunningham*

During my 18-year stint, I owned shelves and shelves of books. Many came through resources like the Prison Book programs, where nonprofits would send used books on various subjects. I also purchased numerous magazines through magazine subscription companies. Do you remember us discussing that in Chapter 2? If you use your resourcefulness to gain access to these materials, you will discover many of the world's most successful people employ most of the Fundamentals.

*If a man empties his purse into his head, no man can take it away from
him. An investment in knowledge always pays the best interest.
– Benjamin Franklin*

In one of those magazines I bought, there was an article called "The Rules" and rule number 2 was "Embrace accidents." Resourcefulness is about dealing with the unexpected, not just emergencies but any unexpected encounter or situation.

The author of the magazine article wrote about an accidental encounter, in a bar. That chance encounter sparked a successful business venture.

He says you can create your own "luck" by meeting as many people as you can and really getting to know them. Each encounter has a 1 in 1,000 chance of being meaningful, but he encourages that those odds go up with each new contact.

His advice and mine on this topic is to meet lots of different people without trying to extract value from them. You don't need to connect the dots right away. But if you think about each person as a new dot on your canvas, over time, you'll see the full picture.

[A] wise person wins friends.

So networking, making connections with different people – a wide variety of people – can be a big resource – probably your most important resource. So I want you to think about the way you present yourself to people, the way you interact with people.

Don't think for one minute that anyone is unworthy of your attention. Don't let your pride or even your timidness keep you from making the contacts you need to be a success.

And most importantly, don't let your personality be a detractor to your resourcefulness. Don't let the way you speak to other people limit your network. If you have an offensive personality, change it. There are a lot of very talented people that nobody deals with because they are jerks. So don't be a jerk.

Think about the way you speak to people. Do they roll their eyes and walk off when you talk to them? Do people avoid you? Do you have a hard time getting your point across? If so, these are things you should be working on.

More Than Just Friends

The magazine article I referenced earlier came from a section of *Inc.* entitled "Innovate." It means "to introduce as or as if new ... to make changes: do something in a new way." This is "The ability and the means to meet situations [more] effectively." It's looking at old procedures and materials in a new light, and it's a big part of resourcefulness.

In 1995, Tom Hanks played astronaut Jim Lovell in the movie *Apollo 13*. It was based on the near disastrous space mission of April 11, 1970. On April 13, approximately 205,000 miles from Earth, an explosion ruptured an oxygen tank in the service module. This caused a shortage of power and oxygen that forced the 3-man crew to abandon the Moon mission and focus on getting back to earth.

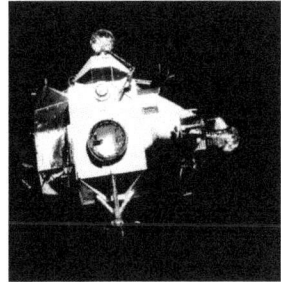

If you saw that movie, I want you to think back to the scene at ground control where the engineers filled a box with all of the non-essential parts of the spacecraft, dumped them onto a table and tried to figure out how to use those items to fix the damaged spacecraft. That is the epitome of resourcefulness.

If you didn't see *Apollo 13* there's a similar scene from the *Big Bang Theory*, where Howard tries to orchestrate a fix for a defective "space toilet" with a box of stuff found on the International Space Station. Instead of disposing of the waste, his toilet shoots it at the ceiling – in 0 gravity.

In the Apollo 13 mission, emergency procedures were quickly devised that hadn't existed before, and the crew used the Lunar Module as a "lifeboat" until just before reentry into the Earth's atmosphere. At that point, the three astronauts moved back into the patched-up Command

Module – the only part of the Apollo craft capable of safe reentry – and splashed down in the Pacific near the recovery site.

I don't remember if Howard ever fixed the space toilet … I think it was still slinging poo at the end of the episode. The point is, in a tight situation you have to use what is available to you. You have to make do. You have to exhibit resourcefulness.

I mentioned the book programs earlier for a reason. There are 20 of these organizations that I know of, in operation right now. I used photos from the books they sent me, magazine articles from the bargain companies, and even a television my pastor donated to the prison to present this material to other prisoners in 2014. Without those resources, I would not have been able to put the lectures together.

The TV, for example: One of the prison groups had a TV that we used regularly, but it took a tumble one evening and didn't come back on. My pastor, Eric Evans, stepped in. His congregation had replaced a TV and had an extra one just sitting in a building doing nothing. The chapel workers networked with me, I with Eric, and we had another TV.

I used it to show the guys images as I spoke, by making slide shows on DVDs. We didn't have the programming to make an actual slideshow, so I used the equipment the school purchased for the closed-circuit education program. The text was produced by a computer program purchased to make the prison's news magazine, and I borrowed other equipment from people who, through experience in dealing with me, knew that I wouldn't damage or misuse their stuff. The quotes in this book appeared on a large screen behind me as I spoke.

There is a silent strength within each soul, and that strength is multiplied for those who remember that they do not walk their path alone.
– Thomas J. Edwards

In order to get the image on the set, I had to produce a jpeg file on my computer and burn that image to a CD. Then, since my standard DVD player was defective, I had to borrow a DVD player that would read the jpeg image, hook that player to my recorder, then record the image from the CD to a DVD that the player in the chapel could read.

So to overcome the obstacles in presenting these lectures, it required five pieces of equipment (counting the TV and the one in the newspaper office) and a network of

> *This book is a continued product of those resources.*

connections and people that took nine years to put together. This book is a continued product of those resources – resources few if any other prisoners at my facility had.

Tell me thy company, and I will tell thee what thou art. – Cervantes

And again, it's not just people, it's not just having stuff; it's having "the ability and the means to meet situations effectively." You have got to have stuff (or access to stuff), means, and the ability to know how to use them effectively. You also have to be able to stretch your resources, when necessary. Mastering the Fundamentals will get you there.

The top pay for a "skilled" worker in a Tennessee prison in 2015 was 50¢ an hour. However, they only paid me for about a half of the time I was in the office (pay was capped at 30 hours a week). I gave them their 30 hours and then some, but in all fairness, I put together these lectures sitting at my desk.

I wrote presentations and produced a lot of other materials that are still in use today, using the state equipment. I didn't exploit the job for my own benefit; I didn't sell my office supplies or make gambling tickets on my computer. The Fundamentals only produce a positive result when they are used in a positive way. Please remember that if you misapply them, *they can destroy you.*

Use Wisely

The use of money is all the advantage there is in having money.
– Benjamin Franklin.

So I found ways to invest my 50¢ an hour. For $25 I would buy seven individual magazine subscriptions, about $3.60 each. For that, I would receive a full year's worth of current, up-to-date information about the business world … delivered every month – 12 issues. That's 30¢ an issue for a magazine that sells for $6 on the newsstand. I can't stress enough the value of these resources.

Resourcefulness is a major Fundamental in prison; it is a major Fundamental in life. It is something you need to start working on *today*. If you are in an actual prison cell, write the prison book programs, request resources lists, or, if you have access to funds, write Freebird and buy *Inmate Shopper*.

You can find organizations offering web services – searching and posting information; buying and selling merchandise; finding rare and out-of-print books. Personal assistants that can handle most anything from typing letters, opening savings and credit accounts, to sending and receiving emails. Publishers that will help you write a book, sell an article or artwork, or design a greeting card.

There are also legal services, (paralegals, pro-bono attorneys, DNA testing, actual innocence organizations who put college kids to work on your case) educational organizations, (reduced rate college courses, grant organizations, even the company I bought the Great Courses from will work with you through your education department).

There are job-search companies, employment agencies, halfway houses. Even public libraries all across the state will help you with research, if you ask.

Finding the Fundamentals

If you are a free person and simply don't have extra money, walk to the library and check out a book or a magazine. Most all the information you could ever want is on the Internet and they have computers there too. Think of the most successful person you know and give them a call. Join a club, a church, meet some people. Whatever it is, do something *now*. The Fundamentals don't work as a theory, only as a practice.

When you are faced with a crisis or an obstacle in life, investigate all the options and alternatives available to you. Who do you know that might be able to help? What do you have access to that might fill the need? How can you demonstrate resourcefulness in overcoming this obstacle in your life? Your success depends on the answer.

> *A resourceful person will always make opportunity fit his or her needs.*
> *– Napolean Hill*

Covenant Concepts

Fundamental #5

I made a comment to my class about being hopeful they had set some goals and were well on their way to achieving them. The classes were roughly a month apart and I had hoped they were beginning to apply the Fundamentals to their everyday life. I was met with a somewhat underwhelming response.

I understood. It's hard to get going, and those who were in attendance had been given a lot of material to deal with, a lot of information to process. Applying the Fundamentals is a big life shift, but a necessary one for every person.

We have only covered four areas so far – four Fundamentals vital for your freedom and success. Even today, I have a long way to go to gain full implementation, so you need to get started right away. These four essentials build on each other – they are successive steps in the process of becoming who you were created to be.

Setting the right goal gives you the direction you need to go. Education and training ensures that you are equipped to reach your goals. Good health removes hindrances to your time and finances, and ensures that you are mentally and physically capable of performing to the best of your abilities. And resourcefulness guarantees you have what is required to get where you are going.

So what's left? What are we to do with all this information? What is the next necessary Fundamental?

My Best Examples

My mom and dad married when they were both nineteen, straight out of high school. Both came from rural areas, both from poor families. My mom worked in a department store and my dad was a shoe salesman. But my dad had something Al Bundy never had, and it is the Fourth Fundamental.

My parents married in October of 1969. Nine months later, in July of 1970, they had their first child. I was born into government housing – a HUD house – a little, two-bedroom, one-bath white brick house, not even a quarter-acre lot. It was the smallest house in the neighborhood.

The first step toward success is taken when you refuse to be a captive of the environment in which you first find yourself. – Mark Caine

Every morning my dad would drag himself out of bed, and he and my mom would push their Volkswagen Bug to the top of a hill. Mom would get in and dad would get it rolling down the hill, and she'd pop the clutch to get it started. And that's how they got to work … every day.

My dad's next job was working as a tech for a dairy. He checked the gauges on the pasteurization process and the Ph levels throughout the process. Later he got a job working for a printing company called Dixie Graphics and Art, where he learned silk screen printing. The only thing these jobs had in common was my dad and his determination to pay the bills.

After working for Dixie for several years, in 1979, when I was nine years old, my dad went into business for himself. With help from a sign painter named "Tweed" and my mom, he opened his own sign company. My dad did the printing and sales, going from business to business trying to make ends meet.

I can remember dad leaving for work every morning before I left for school and getting home late, usually after I had gone to bed. About every seven years, we moved into a little bigger house. I can remember my mom making drapes and bedspreads on her sewing machine, buying food at farmers markets and wearing a lot of hand-me-downs. But I don't ever remember being hungry.

At the working man's house hunger looks in, but dares not enter.
– Benjamin Franklin

By the time I finished middle school, my parents had done well enough to move us out of the inner city of Savannah, Georgia, into the suburbs – out into the country, a little town called Richmond Hill. By the time I finished high school, my dad had 12 people in his employ; and seven years after that, he was able to retire from sign work and move to Tennessee, at the age of 43. He was eight years younger than I am right now (and I'm nowhere near retirement).

I know that just because you have the information, just because you have set a goal, just because you have made the preparation, you have the education, just because you are in good health does not mean you are going to be successful. You have to have the Fourth Fundamental.

The Fifth Fundamental: Determination

Determination takes many forms and is described in several different ways: drive, ambition, hustle, perseverance, get-up-and-go, self-control, will power … it is firmness of purpose; resoluteness.

A determined person is not deterred by setbacks; not slowed by obstacles. Not only is he driven, but he also perseveres through trials. Pushing that car to the top of the hill took drive; doing it every day took perseverance.

We talked about setting the right goal, one that inspires ambition, one that will ignite drive. But drive has to be daily, constant, and continuous – it has to be a day-to-day push to achieve. You can never let up, even if you fail. You must remain determined to overcome.

I never had drive on the street. My goals, as we discussed in the first chapter, were tied up in my evening beer run or my weekly pot purchase. And I grew up with two of the most determined people I have ever met.

Even in prison, I knew not to bother calling home before sunset because there would be no one there. My parents, in their 70s now, still work from sunup to sundown. They are driven by their goals.

It wasn't until I found this Fundamental in prison, that I began to be driven by my own goals. One of my short-term goals was to utilize my time of incarceration to make tools available to those who were actually concerned with success – those who have the determination to succeed.

That was the reason behind these lectures; that was the point behind the *Mountain Review*, the educational broadcast, the *Prisoner Resource Guide*, even the Wednesday Night Bible Study and Saturday afternoon Church service. They were all tools to help prisoners along their way to discovering for themselves the power of the Fundamentals. That is the reason I had the base text for this book; that is the reason I've put it in this form for you. (These tools are still available on our website, CovenantConcepts.org.)

But all the tools, all the truth in the world won't do you a bit of good without determination, without self-control, without perseverance.

Unless you are willing and able to push yourself toward your goals, toward success, and continue to push – all the talent in the world won't benefit you. If you want to be a success, if you develop the self-control necessary to apply the Fundamentals to your life, you have to look to successful people who have come before you.

Finding the Fundamentals

Who are your self-control heroes? We all have these people in our lives – people who motivate us, who inspire us, who encourage us to be better versions of ourselves. And we find them in all different walks of life.

In chapter two we talked about physical fitness and what is required to achieve our fitness goals. One self-control idol that many people have is Michael Phelps. He is an incredible athlete, having earned more Olympic medals than anyone in the games.

But self-control seems to be what's most impressive about him. In an interview he said he couldn't remember the last day he didn't do a workout. Now how many people can really say that? Of course, his lack of memory could have something to do with the pot.

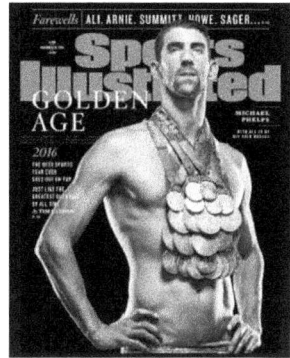

Dean Karnazes is another example of rock-solid self-control for the area of physical fitness. This ultramarathon-man ran 50 marathons, in 50 states, in 50 days!

Now, if you think that sounds incredible, think again. Dean also ran 350 miles consecutively, without stopping. It took him 80 hours to do that. Toward the end of it, he said he was sleeping while he was running.

He's run across Death Valley in 120 degree temperatures, across the Gobi desert, and a marathon to the South Pole in negative 40 degrees. On ten different occasions, he's run a 200-mile relay race solo, racing alongside teams of twelve.

Currently Dean is attempting to run a marathon in every single country in the world in a single year. That's over 200 marathons in 12 months. That's pretty incredible.

But outside of athletics, we can also gain insight, motivation, and inspiration from people such as writers and teachers. A lot of the information I'm sharing with you I learned through a class I purchased in prison.

The teacher of that class, Dr. Richard Ristack, is an award-winning researcher on the brain who wrote 10 books on the subject. He said if he

> *He had to make himself do what was necessary to succeed.*

had only done the things he wanted to, he would have never reached that goal. He had to *make himself* do what was necessary to succeed.

Another outstanding example of drive, self-control, and determination is Dame Barbara Cartland. By all measures she is one of the most prolific writers of all time. In fact, in a single year she wrote 23 books.

Stephen King is another example of tremendous self-control. Not only has he sold millions of copies of books, but he's written 2,000 words a day, every day, for decades.

Haruki Murakami is another example of a writer with tremendous determination. He goes to sleep every night at 9 p.m., and gets up at 4 a.m. He begins his writing, and when he's done with it he goes running. In fact, Murakami is not only a prolific writer he's also an endurance athlete.

But athletics and writing are only two fields we can look to where people exert drive and perseverance. Think of Oprah Winfrey. She overcame tremendous adversity in her life and went on to become not only one of the wealthiest persons in the world, but also one of the most influential women in the history of our planet. She's influenced numerous individuals, in both the twentieth and twenty-first centuries.

Nelson Mandela is another example of tremendous self-control, of persisting in the face of failure, of sticking to his beliefs even when it was difficult. And his determination paid off tremendously, ending apartheid in South Africa.

Finding the Fundamentals

Mother Teresa, Martin Luther King Jr., Warren Buffet, there are numerous masters of this one Fundamental who achieved great success; if you line them up they might look very different. They might have different skill-sets, different experiences, maybe even different motivations, but one thing they share in common is an inner strength – a strength that enables them to override any impulse to give up.

This inner strength is determination, drive, perseverance. It's one of the most powerful inner strengths that we have. So when you think of your self-control heroes, what I want you to do is not only look at the fruits of their labor, but also think about what got them there.

Will Smith said, "I have a great time with my life, and I want to share it." In a video that I stumbled across in the pen I found a montage of interviews he gave broken up with subtitles. In several of them he touched on this topic. Here are a few examples:

There's no shortcut to success: "The separation of talent and skill is one of the greatest misunderstood concepts for people who are trying to excel, who have dreams, who want to do things. Talent you have naturally. Skill is only developed by hours and hours and hours of beating on your craft."

"I've never really viewed myself as particularly talented. Where I excel is ridiculous, sickening work ethic. While the other guy is sleeping, I'm working. While the other guy is eating, I'm working."

"There's no easy way around it. No matter how talented you are, your talent will fail you if you're not skilled. You know, if you don't study, if you don't work really hard and dedicate yourself to being better every day, you'll never be able to communicate with people with your artistry the way that you want."

"The only thing that I see that is distinctly different about me is that I am not afraid to die on a treadmill. You might have more talent than me, you might be smarter than me, but if we get on the treadmill together there's two things: you're getting off first or I'm gonna die! It's really that simple."

Lay one brick at a time: (Steve Croft – voice-over): "One summer his dad tore down a brick wall in front of his business, and told 12-year-old Will and his 9-year-old brother to rebuild it. A job they said was impossible. It took them a year and a half but they did it."

"And he said, 'Now don't you ever tell me there is something you can't do.'"

"You don't try to build a wall. You don't set out to build a wall. You don't say, 'I'm going to build the biggest, baddest, greatest wall that's ever been built.' You don't start there. You say, 'I'm going to lay this brick as perfectly as a brick can be laid.' And you do that every single day, and soon you have a wall."

These are those short-term goals we talked about: Every day you have to focus on getting them right, reaching your small goals, laying your bricks "as perfectly" as you can. Soon you have a foundation to build a successful life on.

You have to believe: "The first step, before anybody else in the world believes it, is that you have to believe it. There is no reason to have a plan B, because it distracts from plan A. I think that there is a certain delusional quality that all successful people have to have. You have to believe that something different than what has happened for the past 50 million years of history, you have to believe that something different can happen."

"Confucius said, 'He who says he can and he who says he can't are both usually right.'"

Nothing is unrealistic: "Being realistic is the most commonly traveled road to mediocrity. Why would you be realistic? What is the point in being realistic? I'm going to do it, it's done. The second I decide, it's done; it's already done. Now we just got to wait for y'all to see."

"It's unrealistic to walk in a room and flip a switch and lights come on. That's unrealistic. Fortunately, Edison didn't think so. It's unrealistic to think you're going to bend a piece of metal and fly people over an ocean in that metal. That's unrealistic. But fortunately, the Wright Brothers and others didn't believe that. ..."

"There is a redemptive power that making a choice has. Rather than feeling that you're at an effect to all the things that are happening, make a choice. You just decide what it's going to be, who you're going to be, how you're going to do it. You just decide, and from that point, the universe is going to get out of your way. ..."

You really gotta focus: "I realize that to have the level of success that I want to have, it's difficult to spread it out and do multiple things. It takes such a desperate, obsessive focus. You gotta focus with all of your fiber, all of your heart and all of your creativity. ..."

Be willing to die for the Truth: "You can't be scared to die for the truth. The truth is the only thing that is ever going to be constant."

Protect your dream: (Scene from the movie, *The Pursuit of Happyness*) "Don't ever let somebody tell you, you can't do something. Not even me. Alright?"

Son: "Alright."

"You got a dream, you gotta protect it. People can't do something themselves, they want to tell you, you can't do it. You want something, you go get it. Period."

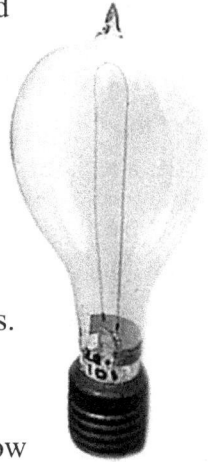

Wisdom of the Ages

Zig Ziglar, another star in the self-help business world (*See You at the Top* would be a good addition to Dale Carnegie's classic) relays the story of a wise old king who many years ago called his advisors together and gave them a commission. He told them to compile for him the "wisdom of the ages" into book form so he could leave it to future generations.

After much work, research, and time, the wise men returned and proudly proclaimed that they had recorded the "wisdom of the ages" in a twelve-volume set.

After studying their work, the king commended their efforts. He was certain that the books contained the wisdom of the ages and all the knowledge that should be shared with mankind. But knowing human nature, the king feared people would never read it all, so he had them condense it.

The wise men worked long and hard to refine the wisdom to a single volume, which they presented to the king. But the king said it was still too lengthy and commanded a further revision.

The wise men reduced the book to a chapter, then down to a page, a paragraph, and finally to a single sentence. The wise old king was finally pleased. "Gentlemen," he said, "this is truly the wisdom of the ages, and as soon as all men everywhere learn this truth, then most of our problems will be solved." The sentence simply said, "There is no free lunch" – and there isn't!

The only time success comes before work is in the dictionary.

Timeless Principles for Success

The story, of course, is of a fake king, but we have turned to an actual king several times in this book, and we are going to again. Even though we live in a world of constant change, some things have not changed for thousands of years. That is why Solomon's words are still relevant today. They are based on a wisdom not bound by time.

This king's servants didn't gather the wisdom of the land and bring it to Solomon. They received wisdom from Solomon and dispersed it to the people. Solomon was determined to be the best king he could be, so when God offered him anything he needed to rule, Solomon asked for "wisdom and knowledge … for who can judge this thy people, that is so great?"

And God said to Solomon, "Because this was in thine heart, and thou hast not asked riches, wealth, or honor, nor the life of thine enemies, neither yet hast asked long life; but hast asked wisdom and knowledge for thyself, that thou may judge my people, over whom I have made thee king:

"Wisdom and knowledge is granted unto thee; and I will give thee riches, and wealth, and honor, such as none of the kings have had that have been before thee, neither shall there any after thee have the like"

Solomon was truly a man of God-given wisdom and knowledge, and with that came "riches, and wealth, and honor," as it often does, if you have the determination to apply what you know.

A multitalented man, he was not only a gifted writer, teacher, and composer but also a student of nature who recorded his observations about the natural world around him. One of his first recorded principles for success on the job, and in all areas of life for that matter, came from observing one of the tiniest of God's creatures: the ant.

"Go to the ant, you sluggard; consider its ways and be wise!" advises Solomon. "It has no commander, no overseer or ruler, yet it stores its provisions in summer and gathers its food at harvest. How long will you lie there, you sluggard? When will you get up from your sleep? A little sleep, a little slumber, a little folding of the hands to rest and poverty will come on you like a bandit and scarcity like an armed man."

Solomon tells us we can learn much about how to be successful in life from the lowly ant. First, the ant doesn't have to have someone tell it what to do. It recognizes what needs to be done and takes care of it. The ant is determined to survive.

Know thy work and do it. – Thomas Carlyle

Any supervisor recognizes the value of an employee with such an approach, someone who learns his job, does it, and doesn't have to be reminded what to do. Those who must constantly be told what to do are rarely successful because they not only drain the time and energy of their managers, but they show little or no initiative or potential for advancement.

My boss in prison worked at the school building and I worked in an entirely different security area, at the library. He had no idea what I did from

> *He didn't have to worry about whether I was doing my job or not.*

day to day. But he knew when a deadline came around he would have a proof sitting on his desk. He knew I was constantly collecting information, preparing for the next issue – or maybe an issue three years down the road. He didn't have to worry about whether I was doing my job or not. Experience had taught him that I was.

The ant in Solomon's observation instinctively recognizes the need to prepare for the future. When the opportunity is there to gather food, it willingly and diligently works hard to store up provisions for lean times ahead.

Likewise, we should recognize the need to prepare for the future. When circumstances are good, make the most of them, recognizing that it won't always be this way. When opportunities present themselves, we should learn to recognize and act on them while circumstances allow. Otherwise they might not present themselves again.

A lot of people rode through the worst of the Bush/Obama recession on money they had saved up when times were better. Trump's presidency fostered another economic boon on which many rode through the COVID 19 "pandemic." Where do you think the Biden administration is taking us? Buy a book, take a class, and explore a new career field … if you have it, the time is now!

The Value of Hard Work

One lesson from Solomon's meditations on the ant's behavior is unmistakable: To be successful requires hard work. The ant seems instinctively to know it must work hard to survive. Too many people have yet to figure that out.

No one wants to hire (or keep) a person who is lazy, passive, not dependable, and always looking for excuses or ways to get out of work. Such people usually are more trouble than they are worth. Solomon points out that such people usually end up suffering from poverty.

That was the trouble my dad had with me. You might wonder why I'm not currently a successful businessman down in Georgia. When dad retired, I was one of his problem employees.

> *Some people don't recognize opportunity when it knocks*
> *because it comes in the form of hard work. – H. L. Mencken*

I didn't have the drive to run a successful business, or any business for that matter. I was still focused on easy money; I was going to make that big drug deal that never comes. I didn't have the determination to apply myself to real, honest work.

You might note that Solomon implies that consequences strike lazy people unexpectedly, like a bandit or robber who strikes suddenly and without warning.

When I finally made it to prison in 2000 – and I had been working on getting there for a long time – everything I owned was leased or financed. Aside from an old truck and a few boxes of tools, everything belonged to the bank. So when I needed money for an attorney, from whom do you think I had to get it? Mom and dad.

Like a lot of people, I lacked the foresight even to see the inevitable consequences of my laziness.

Perhaps you've seen incompetent employees go their merry way, unaware of their behavioral problems until they're fired. It's as if they have blinders on. Solomon even notes that some people are so oblivious to their own shortcomings that they seem impervious to reality.

Are you like that now? I was for years.

> *The hater of work seems to himself wiser than seven men*
> *who are able to give an answer with good sense.*

Solomon adds that we should learn from the examples of behavior we see around us. We should recognize cause and effect, he tells us, to learn what leads to success and what leads to poverty.

"I went by the field of the lazy man, and by the vineyard of the man devoid of understanding; and there it was, all overgrown with thorns; its surface was covered with nettles; its stone wall was broken down.

"When I saw it, I considered it well; I looked on it and received instruction: A little sleep, a little slumber, a little folding of the hands to rest; so shall your poverty come like a prowler, and your need like an armed man."

The Proverbs repeatedly tell us that when it comes to success, there is no substitute for diligent work, for drive, for determination.

Finding the Fundamentals

In all hard work there is profit, but talk only makes a man poor.

Talk by itself, as Solomon pointed out, produces nothing. Good intentions are just that: intentions. "The soul of a lazy man desires, and has nothing; but the soul of the diligent shall be made rich" (Proverbs 13:4). Good intentions without follow-up actions bring nothing. Diligence, however, pays off.

Solomon noted that those who don't want to work can always come up with creative excuses. "The lazy man says, 'there is a lion outside! I shall be slain in the streets!'" (Proverbs 22:13). Excuses, too, are no substitute for getting the job done.

That's a favorite subject of one of my employers. Russ Israel, who owns the plastics company I work for, likes to quote a boss who once told him, "No one ever got fired for getting the job done."

> *No one ever got fired for getting the job done.*

Over his years in business, he has had to fire highly-educated, over-qualified people who simply refused to do the work for which they were hired. No matter how skilled you are at your job, if you spend 30 minutes explaining to the boss why you don't have time to do 15 minutes' worth of work, you'll probably be working somewhere else soon. His story is supposed to serve as a subtle hint to a lacking employee. Still, they never see the axe coming.

If you have gotten nothing else out of this book so far, I hope you have come to the understanding that there are opportunities everywhere, even in prison. They are not always apparent, they are not handed out to everyone, but they are obtainable, and they are the way out of *your* prison. The only thing stopping most people is a lack of determination.

Diligence Delivers Dividends

In Solomon's writings, most translators assign the word "diligence" to the Hebrew word for determination. We might also call it initiative, motivation, enthusiasm, foresight. The word translated "diligent" is also translated "sharp" in several verses. Today we refer to someone as sharp if we think he is intelligent, productive, and effective – in other words, if he has determination or diligence.

Diligence and hard work are the opposite of laziness. The fruits of diligence and hard work are also the opposite of the consequences of laziness. What does Solomon tell us about the reward of diligence – of initiative, drive, and foresight?

> *The hand of the diligent will rule,*
> *but the lazy man will be put to forced labor*

Those who are enthusiastic and motivated in their work are those who will naturally get the promotions and greater responsibility on the job.

If you want to be considered for opportunities for advancement, cultivate and develop these traits. Do your absolute best in your current position to show that you can handle additional responsibility. This is the advice I gave my class:

"It's not as direct a path in prison, but if you exhibit these four of the seven Fundamentals, people will notice. And you never know where the next opportunity can come from, or who could give it to you.

"Don't walk around with blinders on. Everyone in prison is interconnected. If you do something stupid in the Chapel, the HUB office is going to know about it. Do something stupid in Property, Jobs will know about it. And if you think prisoners are bad about gossip, you should hear the staff.

"You do not live in a vacuum. Contact notes follow you everywhere you go in prison. They are the 'official' gossip on whom and what you are –

never forget they are there, in print, in the computer, following you around.

"No one who takes a passive, disinterested approach to work should expect additional responsibilities, or the additional pay that comes with them – either in prison or on the streets."

"He who is slow in his work becomes poor, but the hand of the ready worker gets in wealth," said Solomon. The results of work habits Solomon noted almost 3,000 years ago haven't changed.

"Whatever your hand finds to do, do it with your might," he says in another book. This is wise advice indeed. If we do our best with opportunities given us, more opportunities will come our way.

As king over Israel, Solomon noted just how high diligent, motivated, determined employees can go when they apply themselves: "Do you see a man skilled in his work? He will serve before kings; he will not serve before obscure men."

Read the biblical accounts of Joseph in Egypt and Daniel in Babylon. These men ruled empires under pagan kings

They ruled empires their people never conquered.

who recognized their diligence, their determination, their adherence to the principles and proverbs we've been discussing. They ruled empires their people never conquered.

Self-discipline is crucial to getting and maintaining control over our lives. Solomon compared a person without self-discipline to a city whose protective barriers where torn down. "Whoever has no rule over his own spirit is like a city broken down, without walls."

In his day, an un-walled city was defenseless before invaders, unable to control its own destiny. It stood helpless before its enemies, and when surrounded it was forced to surrender, pay protection money, or fight and suffer the bloody consequences. None of these choices came easily.

In the same way, a person without self-discipline is unable to control his own destiny. Without self-discipline, without drive he cannot set and maintain a course that will lead to security and stability.

He will be dependent on luck and on the mercy of others; he'll have to weasel his way through life. That's no way to live! He will often be his own greatest hindrance to success as he follows his own impulses – one false start after another. This is the epitome of bondage.

Solomon wasn't the only Bible contributor to offer sound advice for a successful career. The apostle Paul offers a perspective that can help us on the job regardless of our circumstances. He describes for us the perspective a Christian – and by extension any of us – should take toward our job and our employer:

"Servants, in all things do the orders of your natural masters (employers, people in authority); not only when their eyes are on you, as pleasers of men, but with all your heart, fearing the Lord: Whatever you do, do it readily, as to the Lord and not to men."

Paul's instruction is simple: We should approach our job as if we were working for God Himself. He says that the Eternal God is watching us whether the person paying us is or not. The implication is to do our best at all times, regardless. In essence, when we do less than our best, we are stealing from or defrauding our employer by accepting pay while not giving the quantity and quality of work we've agreed to.

Perhaps no other biblical approach to success on the job and in our career is better expressed than that summarized by Jesus Christ Himself. He noted the difference between a servant – we should read "employee" – who is profitable to his employer and one who is not.

"Does [the master] thank [his] servant because he did the things that were commanded him?" Jesus asked.

Does the employer thank his employee because he did things that were his job?

86

"I think not. So likewise you, when you have done all those things which you are commanded, say, 'We are unprofitable servants. We have done what was our duty to do.'"

An unprofitable servant, said Jesus, does as he is told. He exactly – and barely – meets his responsibility. Such a servant, Jesus said, is unprofitable.

Christ didn't spell out what makes a servant profitable. He didn't have to. His meaning was clear: A profitable servant must go above and beyond his duty. He must go beyond what his employer expects.

> *The man who does more than he is paid for*
> *will soon be paid for more than he does. – Napoleon Hill*

I told my class, "You've got two jobs today: the job the prison gave you to earn your good days and paycheck, and the one you gave yourself by coming to this place in life." Push yourself, prod yourself, drag yourself kicking and screaming to be the person you can be. Everyone reading this book has the ability to succeed! You just have to have the determination to do it!

The economy swings back and forth, depending on whom we give the reins of the country to. For a while, we were handing out money as fast as we could print it to people who have no drive to earn it honestly, and were throwing it at every goofball idea that came along trying to "save the planet." We recovered from that insanity and experienced an economic boom just in time to get hit with COVID 19. Now the giveaway is again in full swing. The free ride won't last; don't be caught unprepared.

Keep On Keeping On

A story aired on 60 Minutes about the Internet retail site Alibaba. It is the only ecommerce retailer in China, and it dwarfs Amazon and Google combined. The company was started by one guy who had no previous experience with computers, no Western education, and no contacts in the Chinese government.

Visiting relatives in the US, he used the Internet for the first time in the '90s, came home, and told his friends that he wanted to make money using computers. His friends did not believe him, they didn't believe it was possible, and his first business venture was a failure. But he would not give up.

Complicating matters, the Chinese people didn't trust the purchasing process. Years of culture had to be overcome. People had always bought products from local people they could meet face-to-face.

He managed to get more investors, and as Internet access grew in China he developed his own payment system, where money sits in an escrow account while purchasers wait for the delivery of their goods.

When deliveries are confirmed, the money is then turned over to the seller. This man's persistence, his tenacity, his "stick-to-it-iveness," made him the wealthiest man in China.

Many of life's failures are people who do not realize how close they were to success when they gave up. – Thomas Edison

And this is a key component of diligence: the ability to push forward even when the deck is stacked against you, even if you fail. The determined person must be able to persevere in the face of setbacks. That is one reason this information was so important to share with prisoners, many of them had lost everything and were looking at a stacked deck to recovery.

But it also had to be made clear that "perseverance" is not doing the same thing over and over again expecting a different result. That, of course, is insanity. The Fundamentals, when fully implemented, will cause a person to alter their false concepts and accept the things they have done wrong. They will force you to turn away from your mistakes.

If at First You Don't Succeed …

Success is a series of glorious defeats. – Mahatma Ghandi

It seems that people are starting to realize that failure is often just the kick in the pants truly successful people need to get going, people who won't give up, people who have perseverance.

It can also be the missing education we need in a particular area of life. Psychiatrist Gordon Livingston, in his book *Too Soon Old, Too Late Smart*, named the first chapter, "If the map doesn't agree with the ground, the map is wrong."

Sometimes the map we are using is wrong, sometimes the plan we have is wrong. And even though no one likes to admit that they are wrong, if we can admit it, then we can change course. If we can exhibit resourcefulness in our approach to problems, then we can innovate our lives, our businesses. We can be successful – we can be free – if we don't give up.

On Oct. 11, 1868, an ambitious, young telegrapher from northern Ohio applied for a patent for an invention, a gadget he called an electrographic vote-recorder, which he hoped would be used to tally votes cast by members of the House of Representatives. Regrettably, the House declined to buy the recorder. But 21-year-old Thomas Alva Edison was unbowed by this failed business venture, and three months later he sold the rights to his next invention, a form of stock ticker known as a printing telegraph.

Edison was the quintessential American entrepreneur, committed not only to advancing technology – even inventing new industries – but also to securing ample profit for his labors. Yet for all his success, Edison embraced his role as a champion of failure. For the man who held 1,093 patents – who changed the way Americans lived every bit as much as Bill Gates or Steve Jobs would a century later – failure was elemental to the process of innovation. "Results!" Edison once exclaimed, as recounted in *Edison, His Life and Inventions* by Frank Lewis Dyer and Thomas Commerford Martin. "Why, man, I have gotten a lot of results! I know several thousand things that won't work!"

Edison is an excellent example of a man with the diligence to persevere. But what exactly is required of people to be able to dust themselves off and go on?

That ability to pivot is a theme in the work of Stanford psychologist Carol Dweck, who theorizes that perception of one's own intelligence and abilities often dictates how a person will respond to failure.

She has characterized people as having either a "growth mindset," which welcomes the challenge inherent in failure, or a "fixed mindset," which resists any challenge that might be successful. Dweck has applied similar traits, on a larger scale, to businesses.

"Sometimes you're in a crisis mode that feels like something really negative, like a big cut in your budget," Dweck says. "But companies have told me that if they approach it in a growth mindset, they think, 'OK. What's a creative way to deal with this? How might this be a blessing in disguise? Maybe we can reorganize in a way that will be more effective going forward, maybe collaborate with other units in the company.' It leads them to think in ways they might not have before, to come up with more innovative solutions that leave them better off."

We can apply these things to our lives on a personal level. I went into crisis mode at the beginning of my incarceration. Prison is indeed a negative setback. But successful people will adopt a "growth mindset."

> *I went into crisis mode at the beginning of my incarceration.*

What I was doing on the street did not work; I had to "reorganize in a way that will be more effective going forward." I had to innovate – I had to develop a "growth mindset." I had to get a new map, figure where I got off track (or, if I was ever "on track"), and find new friends. You have to collaborate with the right people.

The people we involved ourselves with influence how we see things. On the street, I involved myself with the wrong people. But in prison, I made a different choice. You always have a choice and mine steadily improved as I implemented the Fundamentals.

Have no friends not equal to yourself. – Confucius

Are You Ready To Move On?

Have you noticed how, in these chapters, it always seems to come back to you and what you do on a day-to-day basis? That is what the Fundamentals are about – day-to-day change, and having the determination to continue once you've found the right direction. So what is holding you back?

Some people cannot move forward because of their past. It is grounded in human nature that we put the responsibility for our problems on someone else – squarely on someone else's shoulders. Many people feel when they get knocked down, that they have been betrayed in some way, that someone else led them astray, and sometimes it's true. People will betray you. But bitterness toward those people will stop *your* progress.

We are going to close this chapter by looking at one way to deal with the hurt feelings and resentments that sometimes override the Fifth Fundamental – that stop our progress; that kills our determination. It's easy to tell people they need to persevere; they need to move on, but sometime it's just not that easy to do.

The statute of limitations has expired on most of our childhood traumas.
– Gordon Livingston, M.D.

Handling Serious Circumstances

This exercise originated from Ziglar's book *Over the Top*, and I'm going to paraphrase and shorten it here as Zig seems to get a little dramatic. The advice, however, is very good.

Let's say that at this moment you're genuinely discouraged or downcast; you don't know which way to turn; you're frustrated and at the end of your rope. What do you do?

Acknowledge where you are. Take a piece of paper and write down exactly how you feel. Bare your soul, don't deny your feelings. Write it all down and say, "Here is where I am."

You cannot solve a problem until you acknowledge that you have one and accept responsibility for solving it. Get mad about it, and if humanly possible, blame somebody, some place, or even an institution (like your school, hospital, or the government) for the difficulty. You read that right – *blame somebody else*. That somebody else might be a parent, a mate, a brother, a sister, or an associate.

Now, take action: Vent all your feelings of anger and frustration against the person or institution who wronged you on that paper. It might take two or ten pages to really express yourself. Write that letter, and lower the boom on that person or institution.

Now, put the letter aside for a couple of hours, then carefully reread it, make certain you've covered all the bases, and if you left anything out, write a P.S. or a note in the margin. Write two, or three, or four P.S.s if necessary. Empty your system of all the anger, hurt, and bitterness. Address each issue.

One more time, read the letter very carefully to make certain everything is covered, and then walk outside and page by page address each issue and say, "You did that to me. It was wrong. You shouldn't have done it, but I just want you to know *I forgive you for it*." Do that on every single incident, and then burn the pages one by one. When all the pages are ashes, you will probably feel much better.

If this doesn't work for you, don't stop trying to forgive people who might have wronged you. As you will learn in your implementation of the Seventh Fundamental, forgiving others is the key to overcoming your past. You have to let it go.

> *There is no revenge as complete as forgiveness. – Josh Billings*

Covenant Concepts

Fundamental #6

I had an incident in prison that brought to the fore a Fundamental that I was aware of, but had started to neglect as I became comfortable (too comfortable) with the success I had achieved in the system. Eventually it earned me a bus ride to another facility, so my experience is included here for your admonition.

> *Learn from the mistakes of others. You can't live long enough to make them all yourself. – Eleanor Roosevelt*

At one point in my incarceration, a new evaluation system was implemented in Tennessee that began handing out "recommendations" for programs. The implication was that prisoners who followed these recommendations were guaranteed parole. That always sounds good, but what I hadn't considered at the time was that the system would have to last through my release eligibility date for it to do me any good. (It did not.)

It was also suggested that I could be placed in the annex if I completed the recommended class, but it required me to quit my job with the education department. This began a battle of wills between Education and I, one in which I won the battle but lost the war. (Side note: I also learned here that despite the illusion created by "policies," a prisoner never wins against the system … even if they do.)

In the end, I was permitted to take the class in medium security and run the newspaper in minimum security, but the struggle costs me in more ways than one. I was only paid the class rate of 25¢ an hour, I was never placed at the annex, I had to live in the higher security area, and the TAP program faded into obscurity long before it could do me any good. Surprisingly, this isn't the point of the lesson.

TAP recommended that I take a six-month "Drug and Alcohol" program, despite the fact that my charges were completely unrelated to either. The counselor who taught the class said I came "highly recommended" from Education, and eventually I offered to do her a newsletter for her program. (Back issues of *Discovery for Recovery* are available on the Covenant Concepts website.)

The counselor, Mrs. Langley, was promoted shortly after I completed the class and returned to my job with Education. Her next assignment was over a new pre-release program on the minimum security compound where I was housed.

As we have discussed, over the course of time I had collected in my office various electronics that I used to teach and run the closed-circuit education program. At one point I had a VCR go down and needed another to transfer the old VHS tapes over to DVD before they completely quit working. Mrs. Langley stepped in and offered me a television from her program with a built-in VHS player.

The set worked great, and I got all the tapes transferred over to discs. Mrs. Langley said they had no need for the TV and transferred it to Education. All was well and good, until Mrs. Langley got promoted again.

Her state-employee underlings inherited her position along with her clerk, a homosexual with a sycophant tendency. There are a lot of sycophant prisoners working for the staff. My advice to other prisoners was: "*Don't be one*, you don't have to. If you master the Fundamentals, the staff will seek you out." Butt-kissing is far afield from the Fundamentals.

One day while this clerk was admiring my collection of electronics, I violated the Sixth Fundamental.

The Sixth Fundamental: Discretion

"Yeah, your old boss, Mrs. Langley, gave me that set." There was no reason for me to offer that information, other than my own pride. Within days, there was a property transfer slip sitting on my desk. Prerelease wanted their TV back.

Again, pride took over and I started pulling strings. I didn't need the TV, but I didn't want it taken from me either. I got the library staff involved, called in favors from the Vice Principal, and generally pitched a fit. In the end, I lost the TV anyway and burned a few bridges in the exchange. I'll never know how much damage I did there, but within a year I was on a bus.

> *The discretion of a man defers his anger;*
> *and it is his glory to pass over a transgression.*

You're Doing Too Much

I never understood that phrase. One of the chapel workers, the "rock man" (custodian) used to tell me that all the time. His point was that I had way too many irons in the fire. When you work for the staff in corrections, it's very hard not to anger an employee. It took nine years before I angered the ones in charge, and it was the beginning of the end for me there – all because I lacked discretion, just for a minute.

I had always made it a point not to share what I knew about staff or prisoners with the other. I had seen too many folks go down because they could not keep their mouth shut. And when you get to know the staff too well, you start to realize that they are often into far more than the ones they are there to watch. Still, it's none of your business.

And with my discretion in place, I never had a problem. In fact, the final nail in my coffin at MCCX wasn't my run-in with Prerelease, but a project I would gladly have done again, if given the chance. The point is, had I not extended myself in the fight over the TV, I might have had enough pull to save myself from being shipped. (It should be noted that I had Education replace the TV and VCR, even though I didn't need either. They were still sitting in my office, on an AV cart, the morning the transfer bus pulled in.)

In 2014, I submitted a 33-page report on educational media within the prison system. I had worked on the report for a couple of years and had submitted it to my boss in Education several times, but this year he sent it up the chain, to his bosses in Nashville, Tennessee.

The report detailed, among other things, the benefits of educational television and recommended that the state fund a separate closed-circuit television channel dedicated strictly to academics. The one-hour program we were already running was done through the prison chapel, on a station set up for religious services, and ran a very old GED program. This new station would be set up in the library, in my office, and run a schedule starting at the elementary level going through post-secondary courses. The station would play 24 hours and all 2,000+ prisoners would have access to it.

Eventually one of the "big-wigs" from the department showed up and wanted a rundown of the program. He came in, looked at the existing setup, and spoke to me personally – and briefly. He

> *It soon became apparent that I had annoyed the natives.*

didn't seem to have much interest in what I had to say, and it soon became apparent that I had annoyed the natives.

When the directive came down from "on high," the program was "a go" – but I was not to be involved. It seems that the home office thought it was better that the station be run from the school, from my boss's office, and by the state employees, personally. And they took it personally.

At that point, I understood that I was "doing too much." I had caused state employees to take on more work, although unintentionally, and I was going to have to go. The 3 a.m. wakeup call for the chain bus came 33 days before the station went on the air. They made sure I never got to see it, and there wasn't a thing I could do about it.

Needless to say, my feelings were hurt. The following letter I had typed by a friend, Tom Reddick, who was still at MCCX, after I got my thoughts together on the subject. It was really more a way to vent my frustration than anything else, and I surely received no relief from it. It may also have been the only letter from a prisoner this commissioner ever received with footnotes!

And although it is somewhat off the topic here, please be aware that sometime when you do something really good (especially in prison) you are going to suffer for it – *do good anyway*. The benefit far outweighs the cost.

April 19, 2015

Commissioner Derrick D. Schofield
Tennessee Department of Correction
Rachel Jackson Building 6th Floor
320 6th Avenue North
Nashville, TN 37243-1400

Dear Commissioner Schofield:

I have been incarcerated since September of 2000, 15 years this fall. Despite a lengthy prison sentence, I reach my release eligibility date in 2017. I have never received a write-up, work sanction, or any disciplinary action during my incarceration.

I have completed, voluntarily, every program recommended for me by the TDOC. With the exception of programs that required a change in job assignment, I have worked continuously as a newspaper worker (NEWO) since December of 2005.

Aside from my publishing duties, the Education department at MCCX relied on me to schedule and air daily GED and HiSET tutoring programs on the institution's closed-circuit television station and maintain a current list of prices and contact information for college-correspondence programs. It was through one of these programs (The Great Courses, offered by The Teaching Company) that I purchased roughly eight hundred and fifty dollars (*i.e.* $854.60) worth of educational DVDs with my own money, which were also utilized through the CCTV program.

I have been an active member and facilitator of an Inmate Prison Ministry since 2007, currently under the sponsorship of MCCX Volunteer Chaplain Terry Barr. I was also the facilitator of two Bible Studies there, one sponsored by Chaplain Barr, the other co-sponsored by Pastor Eric Evans (Church of God, *a Worldwide Association*) and Pastor Stan Martin (United Church of God, *an International Association*). I furthermore scheduled and logged seven religious television programs, maintaining correspondence with the program providers and filing and storage of the materials for Chaplain Steve Cantrell. In addition, I maintained and restocked a display of free religious publications produced by the Living Church of God in the MCCX main library. The display offers 20 individual titles at a time.

In 2013, I issued a report on the benefits of educational television, *MCCX Correctional Media: The Potential and Power of Positive Persuasion*, which ultimately resulted in the expansion of the prison's CCTV program to include two separate channels – one dedicated to religious programs run from the chapel and one dedicated to educational programs run from the school. The new educational channel came online March 16, 2015.

In addition to producing the quarterly Morgan County inmate publication, *Mountain Review*, many issues as the solitary editor, I also designed, edited, and published two additional publications. The first was a 20-page T-COM newsletter, *Discovery for Recovery*, which ran for one year under the direction of Unit Manager Melessia Langley. The second was for the Education department, the 150+ page *Prisoner Resource Guide*, a publication of educational, entertainment, and rehabilitative resources for inmates. The guide is updated and published yearly to all MCCX libraries. A PDF version is also e-mailed to all TDOC staff upon request by the main compound library CCO, currently Ms. Sonya Newport.

Despite my dedication to my job and my supervisors; my consistent positive example; my repeated efforts to help individuals in their personal rehabilitation; and my sacrifices of personal time, energy, and finances; the Department of Correction took it all apart in one fell swoop. On February 12, 2015, all of my work came to a screeching halt with the words, "Pack it up, you're on the chain today." No re-class, no warning, no explanation – even now.

At one time, the department, or at least prison administrators, championed good conduct and helped those prisoners who proved themselves repeatedly as reformed men of good character. Now administrators are not even consulted about who stays and who goes.

At the heart of teaching pro-social life skills is social-learning theory, which emphasizes *that people learn by observing the behavior of models and acquiring the belief that they can produce behaviors to influence events in their lives* (Bandura 1969, 2004). Inmates look to their peers as role models, people in the same situation they are. When those models suffer loss through no evident fault of their own, faith that good behavior produces positive effects is lost, and the legitimacy of treatment programming is undermined.

This inadvertent punishment of the model inmate emboldens the hardened criminal, seeming to justify his assertion that the system is designed for failure no matter how an inmate conducts himself, and further breeding contempt for the system and hardening the criminal mindset that programs are attempting to overcome.

Those of us who abide by the policies, follow the mandates, and excel to the point of helping others, are a rarity within the prison culture. We don't prosper from extortion, underground markets, and contraband traffic; and are generally ostracized by the majority who does. To be stripped of our positions, our pay, and cast back into the crucible we climbed out of, adds insult to injury.

Please look into my situation, my conduct, and my work, and decide for yourself if this is how you want those few of us who are legitimately making an effort to be treated. In addition, please institute a stoppage measure at the institutional level, accessible to all administrative positions, to keep facilities from losing what few positive examples they have at the inmate level.

Finally, please remember that there are people attached to these numbers, and some of us have changed. After all, isn't that the goal of corrections?

Respectfully,

Garry W. Johnson

Bandura, A. (1969) *Principles of Behavior Modification.* New York, Rhinehart & Winston (2004) *Social cognitive theory for personal and social change by enabling media.* In A. Singhal, M.J. Cody, E.M. Rogers, and M. Sabido (Eds.), *Entertainment-education and social change: History, research, and practice*, Manwah, NJ: Erlbaum.

Thank you for suffering me that small digression, but I should probably get back on the topic: Discretion.

It is more than just knowing when to keep your mouth shut. It is knowing how to stay in your own lane, knowing how to mind your own business, and knowing when someone is trying to pull the wool over your eyes. You are going to find lots of occasions to practice each.

Discretion is "the quality of behaving or speaking in such a way as to avoid causing offense or revealing private information." It's rooted in the word discern, which is to "perceive or recognize something."

> *Discretion shall preserve thee,*
> *understanding shall keep thee.*

The implications are far-reaching, and ignoring this Fundamental will surely sabotage the rest. But unlike the others, this is more about the way you do things instead of what you do. This one is more subtraction than addition, and it's not always as obvious as is sounds. Are you willing to cut out the following?

Blaming Others

Take responsibility when things go wrong instead of blaming others. It's not as masochistic as it might sound. In fact, it is empowering and highly respected by people in authority.

Sure, the letter I wrote laid the blame on the new system the commissioner had imposed, *but that was the reason they gave me.* You can only frame your discussions with correctional authorities in the terms they choose. That is at their discretion.

But I knew the context in which things went down, and accepting the blame allowed me to focus better and smarter next time. When I got to Northeast Correctional Complex, I took a year to lick my wounds. I was blessed with another job right off the bus, making the same money without any of the headaches. But when the school came offering twice the money I had made before, I was better prepared to take it on.

Bragging and Boasting

No one wants to hear how smart you are, how tough you are, or how much money you have (or had). A lion will never have to tell you he's a lion. Genuine relationships are formed only when you stop trying to impress other people and start being yourself.

Besides, once you have mastered the Fundamentals we covered in the previous five chapters, your reputation will precede you. Hearing that you are "highly recommended," even by people who aren't particularly pleased with your current course of action, means more than anything *you* could say.

The Principal at Northeast made it clear that he knew exactly who I was, and that my position in his department was assured. Even though my previous boss wasn't thrilled with the way things turned out, he never had any question about my character.

Let another man praise thee, and not thine own mouth;
a stranger, and not thine own lips.

Whining

Complaining about your problems makes you feel worse, not better. If something is wrong, don't waste time whining. Put that effort into making the situation better.

I'm afraid that first year at NECX I may have been a little self-indulgent. I avoided the staff there like the plague and wanted little to do with the prisoners either. I was given a job helping a blind guy get around, and I did that and kept to myself. I'm sure by the end of that year he was tired of hearing how MCCX had "did me wrong."

But once he decided to try and get back on his side of the state, I knew it was time to go back to work. A new job had just been created in the system, a tutoring job, and within a short time, I had back most everything I had personally lost – at double the pay.

People Lie

Since leaving the system in 2018, I have taken on several careers. I work as an editor and format books, do remodeling and construction work, run this nonprofit, and consult with and build for the owner of a fencing business. Through these interactions a new need for discretion has reared its ugly head.

Part of being discreet has caused me to excise this section a few times. When you use examples from your own life to make a point you have to consider how it will reflect on the folks who taught you the lesson. So I will be somewhat vague to protect the guilty.

When working with other people, especially folks who cannot master these Fundamentals, you will find that people lie. It is apparently the way of the world now, and it is commonly accepted. *It cannot be your way,* and being truthful (which you must be to master the Fundamentals) will often put you at odds with others' objectives.

> *Being truthful will often put you at odds with others' objectives.*

I stumble across this repeatedly and sometimes have to avoid situations where the truth is at odds with what someone else is doing. Let's say your friend is selling a car. You have been with your friend when this car has broken down on the side of the road. You know the muffler is held on with bailing wire and the transmission has sawdust in it.

Now, if your friend is the type of person that would tell a prospective buyer, "Yea, this car has been really dependable. No, it doesn't have any major problems that I know of …" And then would turn to you and say, "It's been a good car, hasn't it, Garry?" Then you have two problems.

First, this guy is not your friend; he is a shyster, a con. You should not be hanging out with this guy and he should not believe you are the type of person that would back up his lie. Second, you are about to do something that is very difficult, but a must in this situation. You are about to ruin his sale. "No, Steve, this car is a piece of junk."

Now Steve knows who you are and you know who Steve is. He's not going to want to hang out with you anymore, and you are going to be better off for it. And Steve is going to talk crap about you, but you are not going to mention this to anyone, unless asked, because of your discretion.

Now this made up scenario is an extreme example, but you are going to encounter this in various degrees from people you will never expect, until it happens. Each of these people is telling you who they are. Make note of it, understand them, and keep it to yourself.

Also keep this in mind when explaining your actions. Never explain someone else's reasoning for hiring you to do something, because people lie. If they have lied in front of you, they will lie to you. And they will lie about you and even lie when giving you the context for their reasoning. And that is the thing about lies, they complicate everything.

> *No man has a good enough memory to be a successful liar.*
> *– Abraham Lincoln*

I have gotten off in the weeds several times with the "why" question, even when it wasn't asked. I was once sent to pick up some equipment for a job. While loading the equipment I began to discuss with the COO of the company what I was going to be doing for the company's owner with the equipment. I was immediately met with, "That's not what I was told."

What I thought was simple chit-chat turned into a corporate "incident," simply because I need to fill the air with words. Never assume everyone is on the same page, or has the same understanding as you do. I don't know who was lying to whom in this situation, but I know no one asked me. My only comment to the COO should have been, "I'm here to pick up the equipment." Discretion would have saved me a lot of headache.

These Fundamentals are not magic, but they are the very core of everything you need in life to be a true success, everything you need to free yourself from your prison, whatever it may be.

They will open doors for you that you simply cannot imagine. And the more of them you master, the more successful you will become. And if you can master them all, you will indeed have achieved eternal freedom.

Fundamental #7

I doubt you have as much time invested reading this book as my students had in class. With the Inmate Ministry Schedule as it was, it took us four months to cover these 7 chapters, about one every 2-3 weeks. Although this material has not been published before, there are several manuscripts floating around the Tennessee system of what you've learned herein.

I also gave the prisoners in my class lots of handout materials derived from a variety of sources. Now that you know the first six Fundamentals, you will be able to locate lots of additional material if you will pursue each subject on your own. Let's take a look at some of what we have learned:

The First Fundamental: Set the Right Goal

In chapter one, we talked about setting short-term and long-term goals. You have to know where you want to go in order to get there. Your long-term goal is the destination; your short-term goals are the map.

We looked at the goals we can achieve in any circumstance, even prison. And we saw how small daily achievements can bring us closer over time to our long-term goals.

We defined money and the attitude that is a must when dealing with money. And we looked at character issues, and some of the qualities that are necessary to have when determining what our goals need to be, and what happens to men when their character is lacking.

We looked at the preparations one Morgan County prisoner was making toward establishing a business when he was released, his communications with the S.B.A., the Small Business Administration and with S.C.O.R.E., the Service Core of Retired Executives.

We read another letter from an Arizona prisoner who founded the *Inmate Shopper* from his prison cell, and we got some advice from him on directing a business from within prison.

Mr. Kayer eventually sold the *Inmate Shopper* to Freebird Publishers and reinvested that money into another business venture he calls *Girls and Mags*. He currently serves as CEO of that company.

George Kayer's son was released from prison in September 2014, after serving 15 years. Because of his dad's application of a handful of the Fundamentals, his son had a job waiting on him when he got out.

The Second Fundamental: Preparation and Education

In chapter two, we talked about the importance of education and preparation, and we examined the numerous avenues available to anyone who wants to expand their base of knowledge.

We talked about the availability of correspondence courses, open courseware, free and reduced-rate book distributors, specialty magazines, and even what many correctional systems offer. We saw how easy it is to stay current in your field of business or your area of interest. And how you can further your education – no matter your financial limitations.

We also added another case study, that of Jesse Livermore, who achieved the pinnacle of monetary success in the stock market, amassing a fortune worth billions. Yet he didn't have the Seventh Fundamental, so when he lost his fortune and his marriage, he simply could not go on.

The Third Fundamental: Good Health

In chapter three, it was the role good health plays in enabling us to reach our goals and not hindering us in regard to our time and finances.

We examined healthy and unhealthy food choices and discovered what makes them what they are. We picked out the few food items worthy of purchase and the many items we need to avoid.

Finding the Fundamentals

We looked at the role exercise and sleep play, along with diet, in helping us maintain good physical and mental fitness.

And we looked at healthy and unhealthy lifestyle choices and we even examined how people change their habits, the Transtheoretical Model, and the psychological resistance we all have to change.

The Forth Fundamental: Resourcefulness

This is the Fundamental for emergencies. We looked at how resourcefulness can open doors for you and help you overcome obstacles life has put in your way, even prison.

We talked about many of the ways you can go about securing materials you need to succeed, and we focused on building up what can be your greatest resource: people.

We looked at how the lectures this book is based on were conducted, and how none of this would be possible without resourcefulness.

The Fifth Fundamental: Determination

Chapter five looked at the necessity of determination and how much can be accomplished when we push ourselves. Perhaps one of the best recognized Fundamentals, determination, drive, ambition, hustle will take you a long way – in whatever direction you are headed.

This was one of the few laws with many positive examples. We started out looking at the example I knew best from my own life, my parents and my dad's business success. We looked at famous individuals as well. Among them were Michael Phelps, Dean Karnazes, Stephen King, and Will Smith.

But we should note that the book isn't yet closed on any of these people. Though they have achieved great success, just like our first two case studies, tomorrow isn't promised to anyone.

As Michael Phelps proved, failure is only one bad decision away. If Phelps knew, and was applying the Seventh Fundamental, he could have avoided the DUI and pot scandals that almost put him under.

We also talked about Jack Ma, the founder of the online retailer Alibaba, and how his perseverance overcame the cultural obstacles to his success.

The Sixth Fundamental: Discretion

The law of subtraction – when opening your mouth less is more. Here we learned that pride comes before destruction, and what other people have going on is none of our concern.

Discretion can be key to people trusting you and provide you clear insight into what others are capable of. It will keep folks out of your business, you out of theirs, and can help you retain the gains you have made.

So it would certainly seem that if you mastered all six of these Fundamentals, nothing more should be required. Yet over and over again, we see that something is missing. Even those who seem to have it all together often find themselves in tabloid headlines, headed for some type of rehab, anger management, prison, or the grave.

Let's look at one last set of men who achieved grand success in 1923. This article appeared in *Corcoran Sun*, a prison periodical that was one of our resources for *Mountain Review*.

Tough Trivia

Did you know who in 1923 was:

1. *President of the largest steel company?*

2. *President of the largest gas company?*

3. *President of the New York Stock Exchange?*

4. *Greatest wheat speculator?*

5. *President of the bank of international settlement?*

6. *Greatest bear on Wall Street?*

Of course, when I first read this I couldn't answer any of these questions. But the answers brought me right back to the case studies we looked at over and over; it seems to be the norm for the wealthy of this world. The article goes on:

These men should have been considered some of the world's most successful men. At least they found the secret of making money. Now more than 55 years later, do you know what has become of these men?

1. *The president of the largest steel company, Charles Schwab, died a pauper.*

2. *The president of the largest gas company, Edward Hopson, went insane.*

3. *The president of the N.Y.S.E., Richard Whitney, was released from prison to die at home.*

4. *The greatest wheat speculator, Arthur Cooger, died abroad, penniless.*

5. *The president of the bank of international settlement shot himself.*

6. *The greatest bear of Wall Street, Cosabee Rivermore, died of suicide.*

These "successful" men mastered the first six Fundamentals and gained astounding success – but they were never free. They were each at the top of their field, men of status and renown. They had money and lots of it. Yet their lives were still empty – they were never satisfied. They craved more but were not able to find lasting, permanent, enduring happiness. Their search for fulfillment ended in disaster.

Success has ruined many a man. – Benjamin Franklin

What they lacked, what every person who falls short of true success lacks, is the Seventh Fundamental. It is the most important piece of the puzzle; it is the one ingredient that would have changed everything for these men! I have saved it for last because it is the linchpin; it is the key Fundamental that *powers* the other six. And I have saved it for this final chapter of the book so it will remain stamped in your mind. The other Fundamentals won't supply you any lasting freedom without this one.

Traditional Blindness

In Western society, we have a tradition of religion. Men and women across this country still pray to the popular idea of the Christian God. But when, why, and how?

Growing up I was taught a nightly prayer, "Now I lay me down to sleep …" and you know the rest, don't you? My dad said "grace" every night before we ate, and "bless you" at every sneeze. In the US, 41 percent of self-reporting Christians still attend church, and I'm sure a Sunday prayer is involved.

But when do people *really* pray? When they are desperate; when everything else has failed. Most in this decaying society will wait until the doctors are out of treatments, the banks are out of credit, and the Trade Towers are on fire before they ever consider crying out to God.

Why do we put God last? Is it possible that there is a living God who might be a factor in determining the success or failure of one's life? It seems fewer believe that today than ever before.

People will ignore all their lives any idea of divine guidance and help – yet when tragedy strikes, when people find themselves stranded on a raft with no food or water in mid-ocean, it is remarkable how quickly they begin to believe there really is a living God!

It took getting arrested for me. I was an average nominal Christian. I went to Sunday school when I was a kid. I knew the Bible, or at least I thought I did.

I didn't *not* believe. Like the demons James talked about (2:19), I believed in God. I even thought we were buddies. Nominal Christianity made that easy for me – once I was in the club: "baptized believer baby, that's me!" After that, there was nothing I had to do. Jesus did it all, right?

So what need was there for me to continue doing right? Why go to church? Why obey the rules? Why talk to God? Why read the Bible? Why buy the cow when the milk is free? I'm going to heaven when I die, right? If I need God, He'll be there for me ...

It seems the God I believed in was a fictional character. He was basically a long, dark-haired Santa Claus in sandals and a white robe. And in my desperation I asked for His help when the bottom fell out ... I called out to the One who I had ignored, disobeyed, and set at naught my entire life.

> *It seems the God I believed in was a fictional character.*

Wouldn't it make better sense if you believe that there is a compassionate, loving God standing ready and willing to give help in a last-ditch emergency – to go to Him first; to seek His guidance and help in the beginning?

Yet some have acquired wealth, lived luxuriously, and then, suddenly losing all, turned finally to God in their economic distress. Others have committed suicide. Few, it seems, will ever rely on their Maker and life-Sustainer until they feel helpless and in desperate need. Even then, the motive too often is selfish.

Yet, if we are to enjoy the good things of life – freedom from fears and worries, peace of mind, security, protection, happiness, abundant well-being – the very *source* of their supply is the great God! Since all comes from Him anyway, why not tap the *source* from the very beginning?

> *My dear child, you must believe in God despite what the clergy tell you.*
> *– Benjamin Jowett*

But in our day of modern science, sophistication, and vanity, it is not fashionable to believe in a Maker. In this deceived world, knowledge of God finds no place in modern education, and often no place in church – that's one reason why so many people fail.

The all-important Seventh Fundamental is having contact with, and the guidance and continuous help of *God*.

The Seventh Fundamental: The Spirit of God

Now I can feel some of you rolling your eyes right about now, and that's fine. I accepted a long time ago that this path isn't for everyone. In fact, *most* have no choice in the matter at all. Jesus Himself said *no man can* come to Me except the Father who sent Me draws him, and I will raise him up (those who have retained the Seventh Fundamental) on the last day.

So, in essence, what I'm saying in this chapter isn't for the majority of people reading this book. In fact, it's not for the majority of people walking the earth today. Christ said His church would be a "small flock" and generally despised by the world.

But He also said He would give them something the rest of the world didn't have ... *Power*, that's what I am telling you is the Seventh Fundamental.

So why am I confident in this? What makes me believe that this Power is available and that this God of the Christian Bible is the source of this Power? I have experienced the evidence.

Have you noticed in this book there are no horror stories from my incarceration? Sure, some problems, but only those that resulted from my violation of these Seven Fundamentals.

During my time in the pen I was never beaten, never physically attacked. I never had any property taken from me by force. I was never sexually assaulted, never even propositioned. I was respected by the other prisoners *and* by the correctional staff.

I consistently had the best job at every institution I found myself in, and I never sought out a single one of them ... they were each handed to me as if a gift. I was protected in a place that does not allow protection, and I was continually blessed in the presence of people who considered me an enemy.

And I didn't deserve or earn a bit of it. All I did was repent.

But God had to call me first and teach me exactly what repentance is. It's more than making some declaration in front of your congregation; it's more than taking a dip behind the altar. It is realizing exactly what sin is and striving to remove it permanently from your life. It is a total change in your life's direction; it is finally setting the *right* goal.

Then He had to educate and prepare me to reach that goal. He supplied me with the foundation of all truth and gave me the mind to understand it. Then, as I applied what He was teaching me, He taught me more.

Every Fundamental in this book originates from the Bible. What to eat, when to sleep, how to work (read "exercise") is all there. Even the Power to change is embedded in the Scriptures. It's more than just transtheoretical, it's supernatural.

It will require determination to learn this way of life and perseverance to maintain it till the end. Even discretion will play a major role in your walk with Christ. As the Father shapes you to be like His Son, who did "not strive, nor cry; neither [did] any man hear his voice in the streets" (Matthew 12:19), your faith will be demonstrated in your actions, not your salesmanship.

So how do you know if you're called? How do you know if this most important Seventh Fundamental is within your grasp? First, you have to ask, and then you have to be willing to change … you have to be willing to put His objectives before your own; you have to be willing to submit to His authority.

You see, it requires an understanding that what God wants is better for you than what you want. That His thoughts are better than your thoughts, and that His plans are continually for your good. And if you will submit to His will above your own, then He will open your mind to understand what I could never explain to you in these pages.

His book is better than mine.

If you desire to know the true God of the Bible; if you are willing to put His Word and His way of life to the test – then repent today. Turn from everything that is separating you from God and give your life to the One who created it.

And once you've made that decision, don't bother declaring it to a bunch of people. Don't run out and put a Jesus sticker on your car or buy a fancy cross for your neck. Your witness to the world will be your transformed life. Everything else is just talk.

> *Your witness to the world will be your transformed life.*

Open a Bible and simply read it. If God is truly calling you, then you will understand what it says. It will be given to you to understand the mysteries of the kingdom of God … but to those who cannot understand this Fundamental "it hasn't been given." And neither you nor I get to make that decision (Matthew 13:11-16).

So *if* you understand, it's time to abandon this world's system, its religions, its idea of success – and all you want will be added to you.

God is calling people today. He is calling disciples, students, out of this world and into His Church. He is offering you *true* success and *actual* freedom from a world that has been taken captive. You can be free of it now, if you will take Him up on His offer. I pray that you do. I pray that you find true freedom today.

> *The best teachers are those*
> *who show you where to look,*
> *but don't tell you what to see.*
> *– Alexandra K. Trenfor*

References

Chapter One: Psalm 20:4; Proverbs 3:6; 16:3, 9; 19:21; 29:18; Isaiah 32:8; John 6:27; Philippians 4:13; **Page 3**: Ecclesiastes 9:4, Moffatt; **Page 5**: 1 Timothy 6:10; Ecclesiastes 5:10; 7:12; **Page 9**: Luke 6:45; Matthew 12:34; **Page 10**: Proverbs 13:20

Chapter Two: Deuteronomy 6:1-25; Psalm 25:5; 32:8; 119:66; Proverbs 1:5, 7; 3:5-6; 4:13; 9:9, 10; 16:16; 18:15; 22:6; 23:12; 24:4; Ecclesiastes 7:12; Daniel 1:17; Hosea 4:6; Matthew 5:19; John 14:26; Acts 7:22; 2 Timothy 3:16-17; James 1:5; **Page 19:** Proverbs 23:5, NLT

Chapter Three: Proverbs 17:22; Romans 12:1-2; 1 Corinthians 3:17; 6:19-20; 10:31; 3 John 1:2; **Page 39**: Genesis 1:29; 2:16; 3:18; **Page 46**: Deuteronomy 14:3-20; Leviticus 11:2-23; **Page 48:** Psalms 127:2 (Smith-Goodspeed); **Page 50**: Ecclesiastes 5:12; **Page 51**: Genesis 3:19

Chapter Four: Judges 15:3-5, 14-16; II Kings 4:1-7; Ruth 2:1-23; Matthew 14:17-21; Luke 11:13, 16:10; John 6:12; Romans 8:28, 12:1-21; 2 Thessalonians 3:10; 1 Timothy 5:8; 1 John 4:20; **Page 59**: Proverbs 22:1; **Page 62**: Proverbs 11:30b, NLT

Chapter Five: Ruth 1:16-18; Isaiah 50:7; Jeremiah 29:11; Luke 9:62; Romans 8:35-39; 12:1-2; 15:4; 1 Corinthians 9:24-27; Philippians 3:12-14; 4:13; 2 Timothy 4:7; 2 Thessalonians 3:13; Hebrews 12:1; **Page 79**: 2 Chronicles 1:10-12; 1 Kings 4:30-34

Chapter Six, Page 80: Proverbs 6:6-11, NIV; **Page 82**: Proverbs 26:16, Bible in Basic English; Proverbs 24:30-34; **Page 83**: Proverbs 14:23, 22:13; **Page 84**: Proverbs 12:24; **Page 85**: Proverbs 10:4, BBE; Ecclesiastes 9:10; Proverbs 22:29, NIV; Proverbs 25:28 **Page 86**: Colossians 3:22-23, BBE [compare Ephesians 6:5-8; Luke 17:9-10]; Luke 17:9-10; **Page 97**: Proverbs 19:11; **Page 102:** Proverbs 2:11; **Page 104**: Proverbs 27:2

Chapter Seven: John 14:26; Romans 8:9; 1 Corinthians 3:16; **Page 113**: James 2:19; **Page 114**: John 6:44; **Page 115**: Luke 24:45; **Page 116:** Matthew 12:19; **Page 117**: Mathew 13:11-16; Mark 4:11-12; Luke 8:10

118

Recommended Resources

Contact: Discern
P.O. Box 3490
McKinney, TX 75070-8189
lifehopeandtruth.com/discern

Request the
free booklets: *Change Your Life*
Is the Bible True? and
God's Purpose for You

Contact: Beyond Today
P.O. Box 541027
Cincinnati, OH 45254-1027
ucg.org/beyond-today

Request the
free booklets: *Managing Your Finances*
Making Life Work and
*What Does the Bible Teach about Clean
and Unclean Meats*

Contact: Twenty-First Century Watch
P.O. Box 747
Flint, TX 75762
21stcenturywatch.com

Request the
free booklets: *The Answer to Unanswered Prayers*
The Pain and the Joy of Repentance and
The Real Jesus

Covenant Concepts

Contact:

Tomorrow's World
P.O. Box 3810
Charlotte, NC 28227-8010
tomorrowsworld.org

Request the
free booklets:

Biblical Principles of Health
Restoring Original Christianity and
Twelve Keys to Answered Prayer

Contact:

The Trumpet
P.O. Box 3700
Edmond, OK 73083 USA
thetrumpet.com

Request the
free booklets:

Solve Your Money Troubles!
The Incredible Human Potential and
The Seven Laws of Success

About the Author

Garry W. Johnson is founder and current president of the nonprofit Covenant Concepts. During his 18-years incarceration, Johnson worked 12 years in correctional education – nine years as a publications editor and three as a high school-level tutor. Along with his editing duties at Freebird Publishers, Garry is a home renovator and building consultant in East Tennessee. You can find him on Facebook, LinkedIn, Instagram, and at his home on the beautiful Clinch River.

Born of necessity, grown in captivity, resurrected by technology:

THE PRG IS BACK!

The *Prisoner Resource Guide* combines information from the best sources available, vetted through the Internet, and arranged in easy-to-understand chapters! No matter what you are looking for you are bound to find a retailer, nonprofit, ministry, or outreach who can fill your need. Contact information for over 1,500 groups, 180 pages of addresses, websites, and phone numbers to maximize your results!

PRISONER
Resource Guide
Ninth Edition

Contacts for the creative, concerned, and culturally-minded convict

Since 2010

Chapter pages clearly marked with our 22 most requested subjects:

Academic and Vocational
Publishers and Distributors
Personal Health and Nutrition
Writers and Artists
Family and Friends
Pen Pals, Ad Sheets, and Big Mail
Prisoner Support
Ethnic Groups
Legal Information and Education
Youth and Juvenile Offenders
Products, Gifts, and Services

LGBTQ
Religious Resources
Women Prisoners
Prerelease, Parole, and Reentry
Important Documents
Housing and Employment
Addiction Treatment
Government Assistance
Veterans Organizations
Mental Health and Victim Support
Resources by State

Only $19.95 on Amazon or Order from Covenant Concepts direct!

A Prison Anthology: Brushy Mountain 2005-2007

Read the book that brought national attention to Garry W. Johnson when producers of "History's Greatest Escapes with Morgan Freeman" discovered it on Freebird's website! (Johnson is featured in Episode 8: "Assassin's Flight," detailing the short-lived escape of James Earl Ray from the Historic Brushy Mountain State Penitentiary in 1977.)

In this book, Johnson walks you through the origins of what would become the *Mountain Review*, shows you the first newspapers he created, and gives you a taste of his initial days in the Tennessee Department of Correction. Experience an earlier batch of writers and what they went through years before the rumors of Brushy's closing became a reality.

A Prison Anthology: Brushy Mountain to Morgan County

Book two in our three-part series picks up the chronicle of *Mountain Review* two years before the closing of the historical facility and marches you straight into the aftermath:

The old-school guard from East Tennessee's most infamous prison was about to migrate across the mountain to the newly-constructed Morgan County Correctional Complex and clash with gang-bangers from the west. Complicated by a hostile administration in Nashville, MCCX employees and prisoner staff alike found themselves caught in a power struggle by invading forces on every side. The end result changed Tennessee corrections forever.

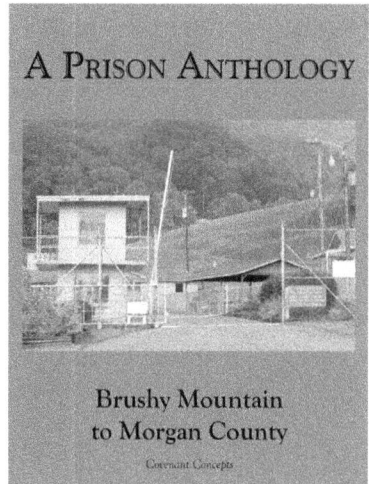

$19.95 each on Amazon

Covenant Concepts Order Form

Please send:

- ❏ *A Prison Anthology, Brushy Mountain 2005-2007* for $19.95   _____
- ❏ *A Prison Anthology, Brushy Mountain to Morgan County* for $19.95   _____
- ❏ **Both** *A Prison Anthology* books (book 1 and book 2) for $37.95   _____
- ❏ Please send the *Prisoner Resource Guide* for $19.95   +_____
- ❏ Please send *Finding the Fundamentals* for **free** (prison addresses only)

Send institutional check or money order to: **Covenant Concepts**
                                          P.O. Box 12
                                          Eidson, TN 37731

                                       Amount enclosed: _____

Full Name and DOC# _____

Shipping Address _____

_____

_____

❏ Yes, I can receive books from Amazon ❏ No, I cannot receive books from Amazon ❏ **Special instructions enclosed**
* Covenant Concepts is not responsible for items returned by facility. Know your regulations before ordering. Thank you!

Please send:

- ❏ *A Prison Anthology, Brushy Mountain 2005-2007* for $19.95   _____
- ❏ *A Prison Anthology, Brushy Mountain to Morgan County* for $19.95   _____
- ❏ **Both** *A Prison Anthology* books (book 1 and book 2) for $37.95   _____
- ❏ Please send the *Prisoner Resource Guide* for $19.95   +_____
- ❏ Please send *Finding the Fundamentals* for **free** (prison addresses only)

Send institutional check or money order to: **Covenant Concepts**
                                            P.O. Box 12
                                          Eidson, TN 37731

                                       Amount enclosed: _____

Full Name and DOC# _____

Shipping Address _____

_____

_____

❏ Yes, I can receive books from Amazon ❏ No, I cannot receive books from Amazon ❏ **Special instructions enclosed**
* Covenant Concepts is not responsible for items returned by facility. Know your regulations before ordering. Thank you!

Covenant Concepts

A Church of God Prison Outreach

P.O. Box 12
Eidson, TN 37731

Established in 2019 by a former state prisoner of 18 years, our organization is a nonprofit dedicated to providing free educational materials to the incarcerated worldwide. We provide one new or used educational book every six months, free of charge. We request that you send us three areas of interest, preferably one from each field we cover (academic/vocational, self-help, and spiritual). To each inquiry, we will respond with acknowledgment of your request, receipt for the book we purchased, a free magazine from one of our affiliate Church organizations, and any additional information we believe helpful. We do not provide any fiction materials and we work from donations, so please be patient. The following form should be used when requesting books or requests should include the following information:

Full Legal Name: _____

Prison ID Number: _____

Name of Institution: _____

Mailing Address: _____

_____

Earliest Possible Release Date: _____

Areas of Interest –
    Academic/Vocational: _____

    Self-Help: _____

    Spiritual: _____

Special Mailing Instructions: _____
        (e.g.: hardcover/paperback only; restricted distributors/suppliers)

Thank you for your efforts to make the most of this time. There are people out here pulling for you!

127

www.ingramcontent.com/pod-product-compliance
Lightning Source LLC
Chambersburg PA
CBHW061735020426
42331CB00006B/1249